Domestic Constraints on South Korean Foreign Policy

D1128977

COUNCIL *on*
FOREIGN
RELATIONS

January 2018

Domestic Constraints on South Korean Foreign Policy

Scott A. Snyder, Geun Lee,
Young Ho Kim, and Jiyoon Kim

MIX
Paper from
responsible sources
FSC® C101537

Contents

Introduction

Scott A. Snyder

Despite becoming influential on the world scene, South Korea remains a relatively weak country surrounded by larger, more powerful neighbors. This contrast between its global rank as a top-twenty economy and its regional status as the weakest country in Northeast Asia (with the exception of North Korea) poses a paradox for South Korean foreign policy strategists. Despite successes addressing nontraditional security challenges in areas such as international development, global health, and UN peacekeeping, South Korea is limited in its capacity to act on regional security threats.

South Korea has historically been a victim of geopolitical rivalries among contenders for regional hegemony in East Asia. But the country's rise in influence provides a glimmer of hope that it can break from its historical role by using its expanded capabilities as leverage to shape its strategic environment. The pressing dilemma for South Korean strategic thinkers is how to do so. As the regional security environment becomes more tense, South Korea's strategic options are characterized by constraint, given potentially conflicting great-power rivalries and Pyongyang's efforts to pursue asymmetric nuclear or cyber capabilities at Seoul's expense.

South Korea's relative weakness puts a premium on its ability to achieve the internal political unity necessary to maximize its influence in foreign policy. Students of Korean history will recall that domestic factionalism among political elites was a chronic factor that hamstrung Korea's dynastic leadership and contributed to its weakness in dealing with outside forces.

One recent example demonstrates how South Korea's domestic political turmoil continues to incapacitate its foreign policy–making. The bribery and influence-peddling scandal in late 2016 and early 2017 that led to the impeachment of President Park Geun-hye generated a political leadership vacuum at a moment of rising tensions surrounding the development of North Korea's nuclear program. Although the impeachment process and subsequent snap elections were testament to the effectiveness of South Korean democratic procedures as instruments of public accountability, the impeachment itself caused South Korea to lose diplomatic momentum and influence over an issue that directly affects its national security interests.

Against this backdrop, the four essays in this volume provide in-depth examinations of the National Assembly, bureaucratic politics, public opinion, and the constitution as possible impediments to South Korea's ability to achieve its foreign policy objectives. Given the country's relative weakness and the likelihood that it cannot fully control its external security environment against grave challenges from larger powers, it is all the more important for South Korea to manage and reduce the domestic constraints on its ability to project an effective and united foreign policy to the world.

Seoul National University Professor Geun Lee examines the executive-legislative relationship, finding that, though the National Assembly provides some foreign policy oversight in hearings with foreign ministry officials and occasionally serves as a megaphone for hot-button national issues, its role in shaping foreign policy is secondary. The National Assembly conducts its own diplomatic exchanges with counterpart legislative bodies in a way that promotes networking and information exchange, but—with the exception of occasional backdoor diplomacy with Japanese parliamentarians—it does not exert extensive influence over foreign policy formation or conduct. In fact, a 2012 parliamentary revision requiring assent from 60 percent of National Assembly representatives to consider legislation increases the incentive for the executive to avoid formal involvement of the legislative branch on controversial foreign policy matters.

Korea National Defense University Professor Young Ho Kim examines the ways in which institutional bureaucratic interests have influenced foreign policy formation under five presidential administrations, illustrating both the evolution of South Korea's decision-making structures and the foreign policy consequences of the president's personal style and preferences. Kim concludes that presidential leadership matters tremendously and that policy toward North Korea is the issue most susceptible to bureaucratic politics. Kim attributes the influence of bureaucratic politics to the opposing interests of the Ministry of

Unification (which promotes inter-Korean relations and pursues uni-fication) and the Ministry of National Defense and the National Intel-ligence Service (which take a defensive and adversarial stance toward North Korea).

Asan Institute for Policy Studies polling specialist Jiyoon Kim ana-lyzes recent trends in South Korean public opinion toward Japan, argu-ably the most sensitive foreign policy topic among the public, and draws some surprising conclusions. Kim argues that the president and elites have a tremendous capacity to shape public opinion on controversial issues, especially among the president's core political constituencies. But the capacity of the president to use that influence depends in part on his or her approval rating and the timing of the decision in question. This conclusion underscores the role of presidential leadership as a pri-mary factor both in setting South Korean foreign policy and in mobiliz-ing public support for those policies.

In the final essay, I examine South Korea's debates over constitutional revision from the perspective of how various proposed reforms would influence the country's foreign policy. I maintain that the removal of the presidential single-term limit would promote greater foreign policy continuity and avoid the need to start from scratch in policy and per-sonnel every five years. I also advocate for strengthening the National Assembly's oversight role to enhance public accountability and for standardizing South Korea's election schedule to generate greater pre-dictability in the domestic political cycle that would enhance stability and continuity in foreign policy.

These essays support the argument that strong and effective presi-dential leadership is the most important prerequisite for South Korea to sustain and project an effective foreign policy abroad. That leadership should be attentive to the need for public consensus and should operate within established legislative mechanisms that ensure public account-ability. The underlying structures sustaining South Korea's foreign policy formation are generally sound; the bigger challenge is to manage domestic politics in ways that promote public confidence about the direction and accountability of presidential leadership in foreign policy.

Strengthening the National Assembly's Influence on South Korean Foreign Policy

Geun Lee

In the United States, two opposing arguments circulate about congressional influence on foreign policy. One posits that Congress, because of its members' relative lack of knowledge of international affairs, has minimal sway over foreign policy decisions made by the executive branch.[1] Members of Congress, the theory goes, invest more time and resources in domestic issues because they produce higher returns on reelection prospects. The opposing argument emphasizes the power of Congress in foreign policy, citing the many ways it can constrain or support the executive using its legislative and budgetary powers, oversight and investigative authority through hearings and committees, and its ability to form and shift public opinion.[2]

Depending on the context, either argument can be true. For example, if the issue is about dispatching combat troops abroad or enacting major trade deals, then Congress will try to influence the policies of the executive. On the other hand, Congress is not deeply interested in technical topics or those that only indirectly affect American interests, such as the protection of endangered species abroad, reform in the United Nations, or Japan's territorial disputes with Russia. Congress will be much more powerful and influential at the stage of treaty ratification than when a new administration is beginning to set up guidelines for its foreign policy. The question is not whether the legislature influences the executive branch's foreign policy decisions—but when and how it becomes influential.

The presidential system in South Korea—formally the Republic of Korea (ROK)—is similar to that of the United States, but the Korean National Assembly differs from its U.S. counterpart in important ways. First, the National Assembly has historically been extremely vocal on specific nationalistic issues. When the executive carelessly or unilaterally handles those issues, the National Assembly has, without exception, attempted to intervene. Second, the National Assembly often interacts directly with foreign governments and its counterparts abroad. Although the consequences of direct diplomacy by the National Assembly are typically minor, the legislature's direct diplomacy bears significant importance in the case of South Korea-Japan relations. Third, the revised 2012 National Assembly law makes the ratification process of an international treaty extremely complicated. One implication of the 2012 revision is that the executive branch will have to maintain a close relationship with the National Assembly from the early stages in matters of utmost significance relating to major trade deals and peace on the Korean Peninsula.

Despite the growing power of the National Assembly, it continues to have only limited influence on South Korea's foreign policy, as the president's office is generally able to get its way on foreign affairs. For the National Assembly to play a greater role, its members will need to seek out the most qualified personnel for staff members, strengthen ties with the Ministry of Foreign Affairs, make greater use of the National Assembly Research Service (NARS), bridge the gaps between political parties, and establish closer networks with other countries.

THE NATIONAL ASSEMBLY AND ITS POWERS

The National Assembly can constrain or support foreign policies made and implemented by the executive using both its legal authority and nonlegal strategies, such as making use of public opinion. The lawmaking powers are explicitly stated in Articles 76 and 88 of the South Korean constitution. Therefore, the National Assembly can support or put pressure on the executive by making laws pertaining to foreign policy. However, it rarely initiates or proposes bills relating to foreign affairs, and the existing laws concerning foreign affairs are mostly about organizational structures, personnel, and budget allocation in the Ministry of Foreign Affairs. The National Assembly can still pressure the ministry by putting up a fight against passing these bills, but in terms of designing, revising, or halting the broader core foreign policy of the executive, its influence has been trivial.[3]

Article 60 of the constitution bestows the National Assembly with the right to approve treaties made by the South Korean executive with foreign governments and international organizations in areas such as mutual aid, national security, trade, war, or troop dispatches. This is a powerful tool of leverage because, without ratification by the National Assembly, the executive cannot bring treaties into effect. Foreign policy planners in the government, therefore, pay constant attention to this approval process. This is the area where the National Assembly has its strongest influence over the executive, and the real battle between the two thus tends to be at the late stages of treaty negotiations.

The National Assembly also exerts power over the executive by stopping or revising budget bills relating to foreign policy. Article 54 of the constitution, which states that the National Assembly has the right to deliberate and settle budget bills, ensures this authority. Given that the budget of the foreign ministry has always been less than 1 percent of the total government budget, and that most of its budget is spent on routine diplomatic operations, the approval power of the National Assembly tends to be limited to relatively small new initiatives such as official development aid and public diplomacy.

Article 61 of the constitution entitles the National Assembly to inspect and investigate government offices, and enables it to demand the submission of documents and subpoena government officials. This authority may not be a direct and immediate means to influence foreign policy decisions, but the National Assembly can delay foreign policy implementation or change its details by disclosing sensitive documents or revealing information that can stir up public opinion. For issues relating to trade deals, inter-Korean relations, South Korea-Japan relations, and the U.S.-South Korea alliance in particular, the National Assembly can directly appeal to public opinion to put pressure on the executive. Those issues can stoke feelings of nationalism and mobilize the public. The National Assembly can also take advantage of hearings to appeal to the public.

THE PROBLEM OF A DIVIDED GOVERNMENT

In the ROK, checks and balances between the legislature and the executive are not as strict and sacred as in the United States. Usually, legislators in the president's party uniformly support the executive and the party line, and if a member of the ruling party independently betrays the president, that legislator may be penalized by his or her party or by the president. That is even more true during general elections, when the president has substantial power to nominate candidates. When the ruling party in the executive is also the majority party in the National Assembly, and the president is at the apex of his or her power, the government can therefore easily make and implement foreign policy decisions. The foreign policy bureaucracy has rarely challenged the executive. The official foreign policy of the government therefore reflects the ideas and philosophy of the president, and the ruling party generally supports the president.

However, if opposing parties control or paralyze the National Assembly, the executive cannot lead effectively. Opposing party members can block a foreign policy agenda that goes against the interests of their political base. Moreover, the revision of the National Assembly law in 2012 made passing a bill extremely difficult even if the ruling majority party supports the executive. According to the revised law, the chairperson of the National Assembly—who formerly had the legal authority to unilaterally submit a bill to a vote—cannot do so except in cases of natural disasters and emergencies. Even when the fast-track exception is invoked, a bill cannot be introduced to a general vote unless three-fifths of the members of the National Assembly (180 of 300 members) approve the bill. Theoretically, a ruling party with more than 180 members in the National Assembly can easily pass a bill. In reality, a majority party rarely acquires more than 60 percent consent of the entire National Assembly without forming a coalition with other parties.

THE NATIONAL ASSEMBLY'S INFLUENCE ON SOUTH KOREAN FOREIGN POLICY

The National Assembly can exert the most influence on the executive during three periods: the transition to a new presidential administration, a policy's implementation, or a policy's ratification.

TRANSITION TO A NEW ADMINISTRATION

Every five years, a new administration takes power in South Korea and announces its official foreign policy vision and agenda. Normally, the broad framework of this agenda is prepared during the campaigning period by the so-called election camp of each presidential candidate, and the candidates advertise their platforms throughout the campaigns.

The election camps are collections of ideologues, experts, and activists of the political party, together with scholars, former bureaucrats, and those who are personally close to the candidates. The camps start preparing their foreign policy agendas long before the election.

After a presidential election takes place, the transition team and the foreign ministry will further refine the vision and policies of the president-elect, and relevant government agencies can assist by providing their expertise. The National Assembly generally does not intervene in this process and normally respects the autonomy of the transition team. In some instances, specific policies have been leaked to the press during the transition period, sparking resistance from opposition political parties. Nevertheless, such occasions are exceptions.

Opposition parties can also pressure the transition team by publishing a report criticizing, for example, a lack of experience of those on the team.[4] Individual members of the National Assembly sometimes try to impugn the transition team with rumors or leaked information as well. In 2003, for example, some lawmakers of the conservative Grand National Party claimed that members of the incoming progressive Roh Moo-hyun team included pro-North Korea scholars and activists.[5] Nonetheless, the consequences of such efforts were negligible. The National Assembly usually does not intervene unless a transition team commits serious mistakes or violates the law.

After a new administration is officially sworn in, the National Assembly becomes an active forum where members can defend or attack the foreign policy directives of the new government. Even at this stage, however, the National Assembly normally acts not as an independent institution against or for the executive, but as a forum where opposition parties and the ruling party clash. For example, when the Lee Myung-bak government in 2008 started to nullify some of the North Korea policies of the previous Kim Dae-jung and Roh Moo-hyun governments, opposition parties and their lawmakers bombarded the government with criticism. Nevertheless, the National Assembly could not transform itself into more than a forum, and the new government did end up doing away with most of the agreements struck between North Korea and the two previous South Korean governments.

In addition, public opinion in South Korea generally supports the policies of a new administration, tends to view foot-dragging by the opposition as unnecessary, and dislikes political attacks that deny the legitimate rights of the government in power. For instance, the majority of the South Korean public, 74.2 percent based on an early 2008 poll, supported the Lee Myung-bak administration's dramatic shift in North Korea policy.[6] The first year of a new administration is a honeymoon period when the National Assembly typically refrains from making harsh attacks unless the executive commits serious legal or ethical errors. Generally speaking, newly anointed administrations have been able to proceed with their foreign policy visions during this honeymoon period, unimpeded by the National Assembly.

When new administrations proposed setting up special commit-tees—such as the Presidential Committee on the Northeast Asian Cooperation Initiative under the Roh Moo-hyun government, the Pres-idential Committee for Future Planning under the Lee Myung-bak gov-ernment, or the Presidential Committee for Unification Preparation under the Park Geun-hye government—the National Assembly never interfered, even when it had the legal authority to weaken the power of such committees. In any case, a committee's influence depends less on the size of its budget than on the distance between the committee's chairs and the president.

POLICY IMPLEMENTATION

A country's foreign policy implementation mostly consists of executing routine procedures to achieve its government's goals. For example, the Northeast Asia Peace and Cooperation Initiative, introduced by Presi-dent Park Geun-hye (who served from 2013 to 2017), proceeded with the routine procedures of meetings, consultations, and various forms of contact among concerned parties. The same was true with middle-power diplomacy in the Park administration. After a middle-power consortium of Mexico, Indonesia, South Korea, Turkey, and Australia (known collectively as MIKTA) was created, routine diplomatic proce-dures followed. Summit meetings proceeded as scheduled and planned.

The end of the Cold War transformed the nature of diplomacy from war-related geostrategic competition among nations into routine pro-cedures of information gathering, meetings, conferences, public diplo-macy, and negotiations relating to economic and nontraditional security issues. These routines are the bits and pieces that constitute the foreign policy implementation of a country, and South Korean presidents' for-eign policies are not constantly monitored by the National Assembly except during periods of regular inspection and investigation. Even such processes do not stop or disrupt foreign policy implementation unless allegedly criminal activities are revealed.

The National Assembly can pressure the executive by passing a resolution strongly recommending policy changes when a government's foreign policy implementations fail to serve the national interest. Even if the president's party is also the majority party in the National Assembly, depending upon the issues, the executive does not always enjoy the full support of the lawmakers and the ruling party can lead a resolution against the executive. One example of such action was the resolution against dispatching troops to Iraq in the Roh Moo-hyun administration. Nevertheless, as resolutions are nonbinding recommendations, the executive typically goes ahead with its original decision, making small revisions if necessary.

During a treaty negotiation process, the National Assembly also pressures the negotiation team by holding hearings, influencing public opinion, and demanding briefings from government officials. In trade negotiations, lawmakers representing special interests try to influence the order of priorities and demand safeguards, reparations, and relief measures. As illustrated by Robert Putnam's two-level game metaphor, negotiators deal with two dynamics: navigating various domestic constituencies and working with another country. Negotiators constantly pay attention to domestic politics and frequently take advantage of opposition in the National Assembly to strengthen their negotiating positions vis-à-vis foreign counterparts.[7] Therefore, the role of the National Assembly during the negotiation process is no less significant than during the ratification stage. However, it is unclear whether it has exerted this influence, except in minor terms. For example, the negotiation team has prevailed over opposition parties on highly contested issues such as free trade. In terms of information access and expertise, the National Assembly can hardly be as competitive as a negotiating team.

On the rare occasion when public opinion is strongly against a foreign policy negotiation, the National Assembly and the media can derail it—take, for example, the General Security of Military Information Agreement negotiated between the Lee Myung-bak government and Japan in 2012. The National Assembly intervened, arguing that it was never informed of the negotiations, which took place in private. Members of the assembly demanded that the executive submit the agreement to ratification proceedings, which the executive did not deem necessary. Faced with denunciations from the public as well as the National Assembly, the Lee administration did not sign the agreement—though the Park administration later did in 2016.

RATIFICATION

The National Assembly's influence on foreign policy reaches an apex when an international agreement needs to be ratified. The revision of the National Assembly law in 2012 made its role even more crucial. Before the revision, the government could pass final bills together with the ruling majority party using expedient methods, as the Lee Myung-bak government did with the United States-Korea Free Trade Agreement in 2011. However, that incident ignited a debate about the National Assembly law, and the result of the 2012 revision made it nearly impossible for the ruling party to pass a bill without the consent of the opposition parties. Therefore, a divided government—or even an executive supported by the majority party—cannot ratify an agreement unless public opinion is heavily in favor of it or either the government or the ruling party can persuade a significant number of opposition members to join.

When the conservative Saenuri Party was in control of both the National Assembly and the executive, its members called to revise the National Assembly law to make it easier to pass a bill. In the last general election, in April 2016, the Saenuri Party initially set its election target at more than 180 lawmakers—but ended up with only 122, far below their 60 percent target. As a result, the government now has to come up with a more comprehensive strategy to pass bills or to ratify international agreements. Any ratification process will lead to more conflict between the executive and the National Assembly unless the ruling party can create a coalition with opposition parties starting in the negotiation phase.

THE NUTS AND BOLTS OF THE KOREAN NATIONAL ASSEMBLY

The influence and role of the National Assembly varies from situation to situation. In certain circumstances, it plays a secondary role to the executive, in others a proactive one.

EMERGENCIES AND EXCEPTIONAL CIRCUMSTANCES

When emergencies and exceptional circumstances occur, the executive typically takes control: emergencies demand fast, efficient, and effective government responses. The executive can blame the National Assembly for delays if it drags its feet, and public opinion normally supports firm and quick responses. The revised National Assembly law stipulates that, in times of emergencies, the 60 percent rule is not necessary. If, however, the government deliberately tries to invoke the exceptional rule for political purposes—for example, by exaggerating a small event and declaring it an emergency—lawmakers will immediately intervene, fearing the return of authoritarian control or the mobilization of adverse public opinion against opposing parties.

When unexpected events unfold relating to North Korea, the South Korean government is expected to quickly respond by following contingency plans while lawmakers are briefed by the relevant agencies. However, because inter-Korean relations can never escape the polarization between the left and the right in South Korea, the National Assembly needs to be well aware of the contingency plans ahead of time and have the ability to debate them.

When emergencies or contingencies involve signing or changing agreements, such as signing a peace treaty or ending the state of armistice on the Korean Peninsula, the National Assembly immediately becomes an important institution, and the executive and the ruling party need to gain its support.

CONTROVERSIAL ISSUES AND ELECTIONS

A few controversial foreign policy issues could draw a backlash from the National Assembly if carelessly handled. South Korean nationalist sentiment fuels many such reactions, and the National Assembly can scarcely resist or constrain those feelings if they pass a tipping point. Policies involving historical or territorial issues relating to Japan, for example, often trigger surges in nationalism that lawmakers cannot ignore. The executive, therefore, becomes overly cautious in negotiations that could improve relations with Japan. This has particularly been the case since the conservative Shinzo Abe government came to power in Japan.

Policies that appear to be soft on North Korea, such as the Sunshine Policy that provided quite generous aid to the country, also give rise to controversies. Normally, progressive parties face backlash against such policies, and they have become increasingly cautious in dealing with North Korean issues. Less militant North Korea policies frequently generate animosity among voters, and politicians, activists, and other public figures seen as pro-North Korea can become targets of the government prosecutor's office. After Pyongyang's recent nuclear and missile tests, Seoul cannot be as ambitious as previous administrations in pursuing proactive North Korea policies. It remains to be seen how the Moon Jae-in administration is able to implement its own North Korea strategy.

Anti-American sentiment is a double-edged sword for National Assembly members. If the government attempts drastic changes in the current alliance structure or appears to distance itself from the United States in favor of China (or Russia, depending on the issue), that tends to generate unfavorable public opinion. Given the domestic political environment, the National Assembly cannot support the executive pursuing such policies without a significant backlash. The failure of the Roh government's initiative to position South Korea as a bridge-builder and an honest broker between China and Japan—the so-called balancer initiative—is a good example. Although the initiative was meant to protect South Korea's national interests, it was misinterpreted as distancing the ROK from its alliance with the United States. As a result, the initiative never bore fruit. On the other hand, if the government looks subservient to the United States by appearing to protect U.S. interests at South Korea's expense, then nationalistic anti-American backlash can prevent the National Assembly from supporting the executive wholeheartedly.

The government, therefore, needs to be careful in dealing with these controversial issues, particularly when an election is near. In the minds of lawmakers, nothing is more important than the prospect of reelection, which could be in peril if they go against the general trend in public opinion. Terminating the state of war on the Korean Peninsula and transforming the current armistice treaty to a peace treaty is a crucial—yet controversial—issue that future South Korean governments cannot ignore. If external powers (namely the United States, China, and North Korea) move in the direction of dismantling the current armistice system, the South Korean government may have to accept the outcome unless stopped by concentrated domestic opposition. Then, the government and the National Assembly would be required to devise a bipartisan strategy to mobilize countrywide support for signing a peace treaty, if the peace treaty is deemed realistic and desirable. To do so, the executive and the National Assembly could take advantage of external pressures to change the views of domestic opposition leaders or shrink the size of the opposition to the peace treaty.

DIRECT DIPLOMACY BY THE NATIONAL ASSEMBLY

It has become common for South Korean lawmakers to interact directly with their counterparts and relevant government and nongovernmental agencies in foreign countries. Friendship associations between ROK lawmakers and those of other countries are numerous, and lawmakers individually organize foreign trips to expand personal networks, collect information, contact South Korean nationals abroad, or conduct public diplomacy. In general, diplomacy of this kind does not directly influence the foreign policy of the executive because lawmakers' primary diplomatic objective is networking and public relations.

However, in a few cases, direct diplomacy by lawmakers has facilitated or hindered the executive's conduct of foreign affairs. The most notable case is South Korea-Japan relations. For South Korean politicians and diplomats, Japan is a unique country among the four major powers relevant to Korean affairs (the United States, China, Japan, and Russia): there they have relatively easy access to high-ranking government officials and politicians, including the prime minister's office. Japanese politicians and legislators take personal networks seriously, making it possible for South Korean lawmakers to have informal gatherings with members of the Japanese Diet (the country's legislature). The two countries have a long tradition of building personal networks among senior politicians. Those networks can function as backdoor channels to deliver and discuss sensitive messages and to deliberate any differences before official meetings between the two governments take place. Backdoor diplomacy among senior politicians is crucial because it allows for candid discussions on controversial issues and is based on trust that has been built over years.[8] That Japan has a cabinet system makes direct diplomacy between lawmakers on the two sides even more important for South Korea because the Japanese cabinet is composed of top Diet members who, in turn, are heavily influenced by their parties and factions within their parties.

ROLE OF THE NATIONAL ASSEMBLY STAFF

Members of the National Assembly normally serve on a specific standing committee for two years and then rotate to other committees.
Therefore, no matter how hard lawmakers study the issues of their
committees, they rarely become experts unless they are repeatedly
reelected to the same committee. Simultaneously, lawmakers need to
spend a large portion of their time in their electoral districts and tackle
domestic issues as well. The role of expert staff members belonging to
an individual lawmaker's office is important in terms of gathering and
analyzing information, preparing questions for hearings, and introduc-
ing bills.

Many staff members are trained as experts on particular subject
areas, and many are experts on foreign affairs either by academic training or by experience. A legislator's staff is typically recruited from the
existing pool of staff members, inherited from outgoing lawmakers, or
hired from academia or the private sector. Those who serve as foreign
affairs staff for many years are well aware of the details of South Korea's
foreign policies and how the government is run, and know important
diplomats and members of the press. Lawmakers rely heavily on those
staff members during hearings, national inspections, and treaty ratifi-
cations. Therefore, having many high caliber staff members is critical.

Staff members simply assist lawmakers; their influence does not
exceed that of the National Assembly. But they often play a valuable
role by discovering problems, misbehaviors, or mistakes committed
by the executive branch. Because the lawmakers are not typically able
to spend time personally conducting research or investigations, able
staff members can perform such duties and present lawmakers with
their findings.

RECOMMENDATIONS

The role of the National Assembly in South Korea's foreign policy is
quite limited because it rarely intervenes in foreign policy–making and
implementation unless the issues trigger nationalistic reactions or contain serious mistakes, corruption, or misbehaviors by the executive.
The National Assembly respects the executive's authority over foreign

policy, and either helps provide executive negotiators with leverage or challenges the executive's positions by inciting domestic opposition during trade negotiations or other sensitive agreements that may affect lawmakers' reelections. The influence of the National Assembly becomes crucial at the stage of treaty ratification.

This limited role of the National Assembly in foreign policy–making and implementation has both pros and cons. Freed from unnecessary oversight and superficial intervention by the National Assembly, the executive can efficiently devise and implement its foreign policy. Because many in the National Assembly do not have real expertise in foreign affairs, too much intervention by lawmakers can hinder effective foreign policies. Furthermore, the relative independence of the executive from legislative influence makes South Korea's foreign policy less politicized and more focused on comprehensive national interests. Because lawmakers tend to represent their districts' interests ahead of the country's national interests, too much intervention by the National Assembly may distort the realization of the national interests as a whole.

Nonetheless, a democratic country, particularly a country with a presidential system, remains healthy and fair only when it adheres to the principle of checks and balances. Foreign affairs is no exception. Timely and adequate intervention by the National Assembly is necessary. To assist South Korea in its conduct of foreign affairs, the United States should undertake the following steps.

- *Build U.S.-ROK bipartisan networks and increase soft power diplomacy.* The 2012 revision of the National Assembly law makes it even more important than before for the United States and South Korea to build strong political networks—and not only with the ruling party in South Korea, but also with major opposition parties. Sharing information in formal and informal settings will strengthen U.S.-ROK joint diplomatic capacity, and South Korea will benefit by reducing the transaction costs of making difficult coalitions. Such networks will also help foster better understanding between the two countries through soft power diplomacy. Having informal discussions and bridging the cultural differences and nuances, such as those between Korea's Confucian culture and American culture, are of particular importance in an age where nationalism in South Korea is strong and America First sentiments are rising in the United States.

- *Exchange staff members between the U.S. Congress and the Korean National Assembly.* The ROK Ministry of Foreign Affairs and the U.S. State Department regularly cross-appoint their personnel to enhance trust and learn from each other. The National Assembly should follow suit and enhance the capacity of its staff by training them in the U.S. Congress for one or two years, just as Congress could do the reverse to enhance its understanding of South Korean politics.

Furthermore, to improve the efficiency and efficacy of its foreign policy–making, the ROK government should consider the following policy options.

- *Hire well-qualified foreign policy staff.* The National Assembly should strengthen its oversight authority and competence by recruiting and training high caliber staff members to follow what is going on in the government with regard to foreign policy. More often than not, the oversight function of the National Assembly does not work properly because lawmakers and their staffers do not have the necessary expertise. Without expertise, lawmakers cannot pinpoint the information they need to prepare necessary and meaningful questions at hearings. The National Assembly, by building close and favorable networks with academia, should seek out capable personnel and hire them as new staff members. South Korea is currently facing an oversupply of college graduates in the humanities and social sciences, and even graduates of top schools have difficulty finding decent jobs. A similar dynamic has played out within the nation's law schools, and lawyers are increasingly seeking jobs that do not match their qualifications. Because many foreign policy dealings occur behind the scenes to protect national interests or preserve a favorable negotiating position vis-à-vis foreign governments, trained and experienced staff and lawmakers are essential to holding the government to account. Otherwise, the National Assembly may ruin its credibility.
- *Increase the capacity of the foreign affairs liaison to the National Assembly.* For the benefit of its foreign policy implementation, the Ministry of Foreign Affairs should increase the capacity of its liaison office at the National Assembly. The ministry's budget is so small that it has difficulty expanding and deepening its foreign

policy agenda and networks. The Organization for Economic Cooperation and Development member countries that have economies similar in size to South Korea's—such as Canada, the Netherlands, and Spain—spend from 2 percent to 7 percent of their national budgets on foreign affairs. Those countries have more diplomats than South Korea, which allocates a mere 0.8 percent of its budget to the foreign ministry, which has demanded a budget increase to more than 1 percent of the national budget without success.[9] One main reason for this lack of resources is the ministry's weak position in the National Assembly. The ministry has generally neglected its dealings with domestic politics. A strong and competent liaison office within the National Assembly would be beneficial for the ministry and the National Assembly because both sides could learn from each other and constantly exchange information and discuss important issues together.

- *Strengthen the National Assembly Research Service.* Lawmakers should take advantage of NARS. The service has its own foreign policy experts, and they differ from university professors in that they are more steeped in real world information and they understand the political grammar at the National Assembly and the executive. By building close connections between outside experts and in-house scholars, NARS can strengthen its own capacity and improve its credibility and reputation. Moreover, the more lawmakers make use of NARS, the more credible and renowned it will become.

- *Build a national consensus on difficult issues.* To overcome the problems of a divided government, the executive should work to build a national consensus on contested issues. When a consensus is solidly constructed, the National Assembly cannot go against the will of the people. The National Assembly should work to build a bipartisan consensus among lawmakers so that they can lead the opinion of the voting public, especially when emotional and nationalistic responses by the people may hurt national interests. Of course, in a democratic country, building consensus on thorny issues is not an easy task, but sincere, candid, and constant discussions will increase the possibility of consensus building. During the 2017 presidential campaign, many candidates proposed creating a coalition cabinet appointment by, for example, having a prime minister from a major opposition party.

CONCLUSION

The influence of the National Assembly over the executive has been quite limited in South Korea for several reasons. The National Assembly does not have enough expertise in foreign affairs and tends to respect the authority of the executive when it comes to foreign policy–making and implementation. Unless the National Assembly is divided, the executive can easily gain its support, and the ruling party rarely bars the passing of a bill during a general assembly vote. With the end of the Cold War, diplomacy has become the mostly routine business of collecting information, public diplomacy, and forum diplomacy, and the National Assembly does not need to intervene in foreign affairs except in cases of criminal activity or other controversies.

Nevertheless, the future diplomatic landscape for the ROK government does not look favorable. The revision of the National Assembly law in 2012 made it extremely difficult for the government to finalize an international deal unless the government constantly briefs and persuades the National Assembly from the beginning of the negotiation process. Moreover, when it comes to controversial issues such as inter-Korean relations and South Korea-Japan relations, even members of the ruling party may not cooperate with the executive wholeheartedly. Because the transformation of inter-Korean relations through a peace treaty may be the next thorny foreign policy issue that the Moon Jae-in administration cannot ignore, the executive will have to pay more attention to its relationship with the National Assembly than before.

Bureaucratic Politics in South Korean Foreign Policy–Making

Young Ho Kim

Public policymaking in South Korea today is open and democratized to an extent that it could be called hyper-pluralistic. The move in this direction is relatively recent, arising in 1987 with the democratization movement and Roh Tae-woo administration (1988–93) and deepening during the Kim Young-sam administration (1993–98). The Kim administration was the first civilian government in the Republic of Korea (ROK). Under its leadership, foreign and security policy–making became more transparent and open to debate than ever before.

An open policymaking process carries with it the risk of political gridlock or infighting. The concept of bureaucratic politics was largely formulated in Graham Allison's seminal work, *Essence of Decision: Explaining the Cuban Missile Crisis* (1971). Bureaucratic politics was suggested as one of three decision-making models, along with the rational choice and organizational process models, and it emphasizes the influence of government officials in foreign policy–making. Allison demonstrated that policymaking does not always involve making a choice based on a cost-benefit analysis (the rational choice model) or the proper application of standard operational procedures (the organizational process model). Instead, policy is sometimes a result of fierce "competition, negotiation, and bargaining" among bureaucrats who prioritize their personal and organizational interests over the national interest. According to Allison, a policy can be an outcome of "pulling and hauling among different bureaucrats" rather than of rational deliberation or organizational process.[1]

These competitions and compromises, however, are not easily revealed to or observed by people outside government. Developing policy options based on differing views and holding debates about those views are all part of a normal, healthy process in a vibrant democratic government. The existence of different positions or of competition across ministries is not always a sign of bureaucratic politics.

Scholarly attention to bureaucratic politics in the ROK is surprisingly scant. Only a handful of serious studies exists.[2] Given the difficulty of collecting reliable information on the internal dynamics of decision-making processes, this shortage is understandable. Considering bureaucratic politics' wide scope and significant consequences for security and foreign policy–making, however, this phenomenon deserves more scholarly attention and analysis.

INDICATORS OF BUREAUCRATIC POLITICS IN POLICYMAKING

According to political scientists, bureaucratic politics can be identified in five situations.[3] The first is when a president's policy preference is refuted, ignored, or replaced by that of a ministry or a group of ministries and agencies. Under a presidential system, the power of the president tends to dominate, particularly in the foreign and security policy areas, because the president represents the sovereign power of the state externally. Thus, a policy decision that is significantly different from the president's usual preference and closer to the preferences of certain ministries or agencies could be evidence of bureaucratic politics.

The second is when a policy decision reflects a compromise between the most powerful ministers or heads of agencies rather than proper coordination among all centers of power. In that situation, the role of the president tends to be minimized because the president either has less interest in the issue or considers it less important.

The third is if parochial interests are detected or revealed in a decision. In a healthy policymaking process, various options are suggested and contested. What matters is where the differences originate. Different perspectives or views among policymakers do not necessarily indicate bureaucratic politics, but an emphasis on personal or organizational priorities in a decision can be an indicator.

The fourth is an unusually lengthy or delayed decision-making process. Slow decision-making or legislative gridlock occur in the legislative bodies of many democratic countries for any number of reasons. Such delays as bureaucrats negotiate over their specific departmental or personal agendas are a sign of bureaucratic politics.

The fifth relies on the nation's media. The role of the news media is critical: bureaucratic friction can be exposed by either diligent journalism or intentional leaks. From time to time, bureaucrats use the media as an instrument to influence public opinion or win advantage for their agenda, revealing the existence of bureaucratic politics as they do so.

INFLUENCING FACTORS OF BUREAUCRATIC POLITICS IN SOUTH KOREA

Three major factors influence bureaucratic politics in South Korea: the president's leadership style, differences among the ministries and agencies participating in decision-making, and the organizational structures of the offices in the executive charged with managing foreign and security matters.

PRESIDENTIAL LEADERSHIP STYLE

As in many advanced democratic countries, every president in South Korea has reorganized the structure of the government after taking office. This usually involves restructuring government ministries and agencies, as well as the secretarial offices within the Blue House (the home of the executive branch). Such changes indicate the administration's policy priorities and how communication and consultation will be conducted.

One way to understand the changes made by each administration is to view them in light of the president's leadership style. A president who cherishes procedure will prefer formalized channels of communication. A president who prioritizes policy details and actively seeks advice from aides or advisors will prefer more open communication. Leadership styles clearly influence communication styles and channels among government officials.

The political scientist Alexander George identifies three styles of communication in government bureaucracies.[4] The first is formalistic: a hierarchical system with a clear division of roles and well-defined standard operating procedures in decision-making. A line of communication is organized in an orderly and closed way, according to which ideas and information move only through formal channels. The second type is competitive: a more open and flexible system. Views and options can be proposed and discussed. Input from outside the government is permitted and even encouraged. The third type is collegial (cooperative): an eclectic or combined system that allows a free flow of information and ideas but nonetheless prevents chaos.

MISSIONS OF MINISTRIES AND AGENCIES

The fundamental differences among the missions of the ministries and agencies involved in foreign and security policy–making can lead to bureaucratic politics. Different ministries by definition often propose different ways of tackling the same problem. In the United States, for example, this distinction is embodied by the different approaches of the Departments of State and Defense. In a conflict situation, State tends to prefer dialogue and diplomatic options; Defense, though usually cautious, will use force if necessary. These differences stem from varying strategies or methods in pursuit of a shared goal. Differences of this type are reconcilable and sometimes complementary. In South Korea, however, the situation is more complex; in many cases, disagreements result from agencies' different goals or perspectives.[5] Many significant differences can be traced to two factors—the division of the country after the Korean War and the U.S.-ROK alliance.

First, South Korea considers unification to be one of its most important national tasks. Accordingly, it created the Ministry of Unification (MOU). In pursuing its mission of peaceful unification, the MOU aims to work with, rather than contain, North Korea and prefers dialogue, exchanges, and cooperation to pressure and sanctions. This tendency is intensified when its minister, regardless of the presidential administration, is sympathetic to such policies. At the same time, sixty years of military confrontation with North Korea have led institutions such as the Ministry of National Defense (MND) and National Information Service (NIS) to take harsher policy stances.[6] Their organizational goals are largely to defeat, change, or even collapse the North Korean regime. This stark contrast between MOU and MND/NIS can contribute to fierce competition and friction in devising South Korea's foreign and security policies.

Second, the U.S.-ROK alliance significantly affects some ministries, particularly the MND and the Ministry of Foreign Affairs (MFA). The United States, in addition to having fought in the Korean War, has played an essential role in defending South Korea against North Korean threats for nearly seventy years. The military-to-military cooperation is so intertwined that all major South Korean defense policy decisions have been made only after some form of consultation with the United States. Foreign policy–making is also affected by the alliance relationship. Alliance-first thinking is not a structural factor, but it influences policymaking processes as if it were one because it is so deeply embedded in the reasoning of both ministries.[7] It thus conditions interagency frictions and to some extent bureaucratic politics in South Korea as well.

ORGANIZATION OF THE PRESIDENTIAL OFFICE

Another factor that plays into South Korean foreign and security policy–making is the organization of the presidential office in charge of foreign and security affairs. Cabinet members in many democracies commonly compete with presidential or prime ministerial staff over policy decisions. In the United States, for example, the secretaries of state and defense and the national security advisor frequently differ in their views. South Korea, however, has an additional dimension inside the Blue House: the institutional arrangement between the office of national security advisor and chief secretary to the president for foreign and security affairs, which are sometimes combined and other times separate.[8]

Given South Korea's confrontation with North Korea, the role of the security affairs advisor has been emphasized since Kim Young-sam's administration. At that time, the functions of the National Security Council (NSC) were also expanded and strengthened. It is convened infrequently, however, because the president must preside over it. The Standing Committee of the National Security Council was therefore created for the heads of the departments of foreign affairs, defense, unification, and information and the security advisor to review pending national security issues and make recommendations to the president. Offices responsible for functions such as policy planning and coordination were established within the NSC. One problem with the expanded NSC role is the occasional frictions or redundancies between it and the office of chief secretary to the president for foreign and security affairs.

HISTORICAL REVIEW

Since the transition to democracy in South Korea and the election of Kim Young-sam as the country's first civilian president, the evolution of bureaucratic politics in South Korea has moved through several stages.

KIM YOUNG-SAM ADMINISTRATION (1993–98)

Kim Young-sam was elected president in December 1992 after having led—along with fellow opposition leader Kim Dae-jung—a long and difficult democratization movement. He was a charismatic leader with a strong will, well-known for making decisions by relying on intuition and instinct more than advice. Because he preferred subordinates to make informal and direct reports to him with no one else present, no formal mechanisms were used for discussions or policy coordination among high-level decision-makers.[9] The Ministerial Meeting for Security Affairs was a coordinating body at the ministerial level, but was held only on an ad hoc basis (figure 1). Kim had a strong sense of efficacy, was confident about his ability to control bureaucrats as well as advisors, and paid little attention to conflicts among ministers and agencies. His leadership style was thus a competitive one in which ministries and agencies could present their views freely to him, even though he made the final decisions on significant matters. His administration, then, was prone to bureaucratic politics.[10]

The main departments in the Kim Young-sam administration's foreign and security policy–making team were the MOU, MFA, and NIS. The status and power of the NIS, however, was greatly reduced from the authoritarian era before 1987, when it had been a powerful organization with a large budget and considerable manpower. The MOU rose in its place. However, despite having been elevated to a deputy prime minister level two years before Kim Young-sam came to power, the minister had little political support. Only in the Kim Young-sam administration did the MOU begin to be seen as a central decider for North Korean policy, an unusual situation that opened the door to bureaucratic conflict between the MOU and the NIS.

The MOU emphasized a nationalistic approach based on inter-Korean reconciliation and cooperation—the opposite of the MFA's international perspective. Led by Han Sung-joo, the Ministry of

FIGURE 1. ORGANIZATIONAL STRUCTURE OF THE KIM YOUNG-
SAM BLUE HOUSE

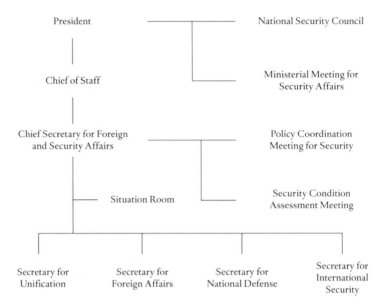

Foreign Affairs took a moderate policy line and advocated close cooperation and consultation with international actors. Such radically different outlooks made bureaucratic politics likely.

One of the most revealing examples of bureaucratic politics during the
Kim Young-sam administration was Seoul's reaction to the first North
Korean nuclear crisis, which began when North Korea announced its
plans to withdraw from the Nuclear Nonproliferation Treaty in March
1993. North Korea agreed to defer its withdrawal in exchange for U.S.
pledges to respect its sovereignty, the principle of noninterference, and
peaceful unification of the Korean Peninsula. The moderate MFA and
MOU responded positively to this agreement, and the hard-liner security advisor, NIS, and MND complained.

This difference between moderates and hard-liners continued until
the Geneva framework agreement—formally, the Agreed Framework
between the United States of America and the Democratic People's
Republic of Korea—was signed on October 21, 1994. The moderates
advocated the U.S.-led international approach and the hard-liners
insisted on a parallel pursuit of inter-Korean dialogue along with the

U.S.-North Korea negotiations. Regarding North Korea's resistance to a special International Atomic Energy Agency inspection, the moderates were more lenient and flexible, including on the method of inspection.

Overall, bureaucratic politics were prevalent during the Kim Young-sam administration because of the president's encouragement of competition among officials, the rivalries between MOU and NIS, and a lack of interagency coordination mechanisms.

KIM DAE-JUNG ADMINISTRATION (1998–2003)

President Kim Dae-jung was also a strong, charismatic leader. Unlike his predecessor, who relied on intuition and insights, however, Kim Dae-jung was a diligent reader and deep thinker. He also delegated decision-making powers to his staff and cabinet members more often than Kim Young-sam had done. Kim Dae-jung's leadership style was largely a mix of competitive and formalistic, though the ratio shifted from one policy area to another.

The formalistic element was stronger in foreign and security policy because Lim Dong-won, the first chief secretary to the president for foreign and security affairs in the Kim Dae-jung administration, controlled policymaking in those areas. Lim was able to earn Kim's trust because he had been central in formulating the trademark policy of unification, the Sunshine Policy. Even though they were distinct in theory, there was overlap between the president's office and the National Security Council in the Kim Dae-jung Blue House (figure 2). Lim was in charge of the NSC while at the same time working in the president's office. All information and ideas related to foreign and security policies had to pass through Lim's desk before going on to the president. Bureaucratic politics were therefore less frequent, especially early in Kim Dae-jung's term.[11]

Less frequent does not mean absent entirely, however. One example of bureaucratic politics during the Kim Dae-jung era was the failure to purchase a Russian-made submarine in 2000.[12] Under pressure from Russia to buy its submarines, the Kim Dae-jung administration initially gave the offer serious consideration. Kim Dae-jung himself thought it could be a good opportunity to enlist Russia's endorsement of the Sunshine Policy. Both the MFA and the NIS saw an opportunity to recover a relationship with Russia that had become awkward after an incident in which diplomats were expelled from both countries in 1998. Even

FIGURE 2. ORGANIZATIONAL STRUCTURE OF THE KIM DAE-JUNG BLUE HOUSE

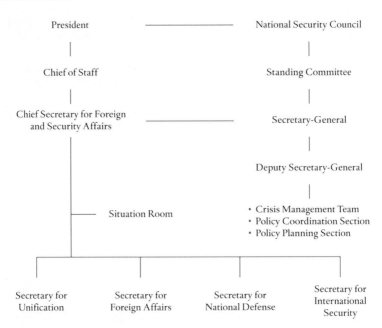

the Ministry of Finance and Economy was positive, seeing Russia's redemption in kind for an unpaid loan. The South Korean Navy, however, considered the submarine as impeding its organizational interests and expressed a strong objection to the purchase on technical grounds. These protests managed to win over the president and others, and the deal fell through.

ROH MOO-HYUN ADMINISTRATION (2003–2008)

As his life's story—a vocational high school graduate, human rights defense lawyer, and opposition party National Assembly member—reveals, President Roh Moo-hyun was self-motivated. He was also fond of free discussions and adept at debate. He believed in horizontal leadership, and divided foreign affairs and security policy among several advisors and the NSC (figure 3). Roh insisted on eradicating authoritarian tendencies in the South Korean presidency, and did not hesitate in delegating when possible. He was also open to new ideas and disliked

FIGURE 3. ORGANIZATIONAL STRUCTURE OF THE ROH
MOO-HYUN EARLY BLUE HOUSE

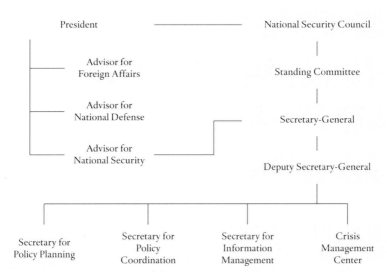

formality, but wanted to run his government according to a rules-based system rather than personalized arbitration. Similar to Kim Dae-jung, Roh's leadership style was a mix of competitive and formalistic.[13] In foreign and security policy, it was closer to formalistic because of his reliance on Lee Jong-seok, the first Roh administration deputy secretary-general of the NSC. Although his formal position was not as dominant as Lee Dong-won's had been, he was in complete control over both the decision-making and implementation processes because he had the full support of the president.

The overt dominance of Lee Jong-seok's NSC, however, led to complaints and resistance from other ministries and agencies involved in foreign and security policy–making. Among them, the Ministry of Foreign Affairs was the strongest. The North Korean nuclear problem had become a multilateral issue, and logically the MFA should have had the leading role in tackling it. In reality, however, the NSC determined the policies and tasked the MFA with implementation, upsetting MFA diplomats.

Some incidents during the Roh Moo-hyun administration could be interpreted as bureaucratic politics, but most friction arose from ideological differences, mainly between the group that prioritized the alliance with the United States and the group that prioritized autonomy. This line of demarcation characterized the administration. A prime example of such friction was the protracted debate over sending troops to Iraq. The alliance-first group—represented by the Ministries of Foreign Affairs and Defense, the security advisor, and both the advisors of foreign affairs and national defense—strongly supported sending troops to Iraq, but the final decision reflected Lee Jong-seok's autonomy-first group, which preferred a limited dispatch.

LEE MYUNG-BAK ADMINISTRATION (2008–2013)

As a successful self-made man and CEO of one of the largest business conglomerates in South Korea, President Lee Myung-bak was a leader with a strong will and considerable self-motivation. Confident in his own judgment, he emphasized getting things done, tended to trust only his close aides and members of his inner circle, and rarely delegated power to advisors or ministers. Putting high value on efficiency, practicality, and field-oriented action, he preferred a smaller government and a compact decision-making structure. Lee's leadership style was thus competitive and similar in some respects to Kim Young-sam's. The difference between the two is that Lee was more of an elitist and Kim was more of a populist. Bureaucratic politics in the Lee Myung-bak administration were less frequent than in the Kim Young-sam administration.

The Lee administration dramatically streamlined its operations, including in foreign and security policy (figure 4). The NSC role was minimized, the secretaries in the Blue House reorganized into a single structure, and the security advisor relegated under the chief of staff.

Lee's leaner Blue House meant that ministries and agencies were more autonomous than before. In the foreign affairs and security domains, the Ministry of Foreign Affairs had a dominant role given the administration's slogans, Global Korea and middle-power diplomacy. The National Information Service also regained some of its earlier power as the incidence of terrorism, industrial espionage, and cybersecurity threats increased. Correspondingly, the status and role of the Ministry of Unification were dramatically reduced.

Despite the lack of institutional mechanisms for coordination, bureaucratic politics were not significant during the Lee administration for two reasons. The first was the extended security conditions in response to ongoing North Korean provocations. The killing of a South

FIGURE 4. ORGANIZATIONAL STRUCTURE OF THE LEE
MYUNG-BAK EARLY BLUE HOUSE

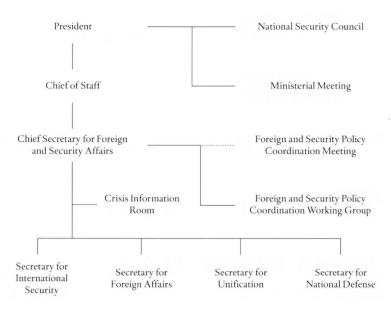

Korean tourist in a Kumgang Mountain resort in 2008, the sinking of
the ROKS *Cheonan* and the shelling of Yeonpyeong Island in 2010, the
death of Kim Jong-il in 2011, and a North Korean long-range missile
launch in 2012 increased tensions and kept inter-Korean relations under
continual strain. Such a situation made it difficult for moderates in the
government to push their agendas against the Lee administration's
hard-line policy toward the North. Bureaucratic politics were unlikely.

The second reason was that most high-level foreign and security
policy appointees had a common conservative ideological view. The
hard-liner Hyun In-taek, who had worked for Lee Myung-bak during
the presidential campaign as minister of unification, is a case in point.
His appointment helped prevent resistance to and within the ministry
and thus reduced the opportunities for bureaucratic politics. An epi-
sode in the Ministry of National Defense in 2009 revealed a lack of
coordination rather than interagency rivalry. The minister at the time,
Lee Sang-hee, had secured the president's approval on a defense reform
budget, which the president later replaced with another by the vice minister, Chang Soo-man, who was close to the president. The revised

budget included more cuts, evidence of the extent to which Lee personally focused on the budget.

PARK GEUN-HYE ADMINISTRATION (2013–2017)

President Park Geun-hye appeared calm and moderate but was a stern
and determined decision-maker. Once a decision was made, she was
reluctant to change her mind, which explains why she was often described
as a person who valued principles and trust.[14] She also had a keen instinct
for playing and winning political power games, which she likely learned
in her twenties while acting as the first lady in place of her mother (who
had been killed by a North Korean assassin). In that capacity, she also had
an excellent opportunity to closely observe the sometimes fierce power
struggles in her father's administration and to learn how to wield power
and treat subordinates. Park Geun-hye rarely delegated her power and
disliked overt competition and controversy among bureaucrats.[15]

Her leadership style, then, was formalistic. Access to the president
was through established channels only. Policy recommendations, after
coordination among relevant ministries and agencies, moved the same
way. If judging only from presidential leadership style, little room was
left for bureaucratic politics; criticism about a lack of communication
inside and outside the administration was harsh, however.

The Park administration started with a dual organizational structure for foreign and security affairs, which was arranged like a slightly
modified version of the Lee Myung-bak administration in 2011 (figure 5).
Maintaining the same overall structure, the Park administration elevated
the Office of Crisis Management into the Office of National Security,
which covered all the security matters related to North Korea, including
nuclear issues and crises sparked by North Korean provocations.

North Korea's nuclear program and missile development efforts
represented South Korea's most pressing security and foreign policy
challenges. Dividing the responsibilities for these matters across
offices—the Office of National Security and the Office of Chief Secretary for Foreign and Security Affairs—was confusing enough to open
the door to competition and redundancy between them. The built-in
institutional linkage between the two offices to prevent such problems—appointing the chief secretary for foreign and security affairs as
the deputy director of national security—was not enough on its own.
Complicating the confusion and inefficiency, the dual organizational

FIGURE 5. ORGANIZATIONAL STRUCTURE OF THE PARK GEUN-HYE EARLY BLUE HOUSE

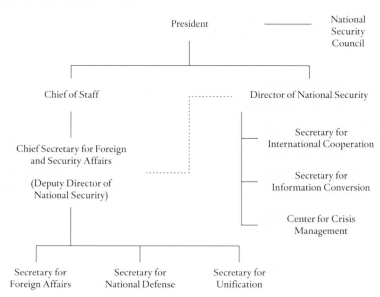

arrangement itself contributed to the poor coordination between the Blue House and ministries and agencies.

To remedy problems such as poor interagency coordination (arising from the dual institutional arrangement) and to improve crisis management capabilities as the security situation worsened (after the execution of Jang Song-thaek in North Korea), the Park administration reorganized the Blue House in its second year (figure 6). The NSC Standing Committee, chaired by the director of national security, was reestablished and convened regularly to discuss pending foreign and security policy issues and offer recommendations to the president. The position of the first deputy secretary of national security, who served simultaneously as NSC secretary-general, was created to manage NSC Standing Committee operations. The Office of National Security was enlarged with the addition of the Office of Security Strategy for longer-term planning and strengthened by the national security director's tighter and more direct control over secretaries under the chief secretary for foreign and security affairs. Interagency coordination among the Blue House, ministries, and agencies, as well as within the Blue House, was improved and the likelihood of bureaucratic politics reduced.

FIGURE 6. REORGANIZED STRUCTURE OF THE PARK GEUN-HYE BLUE HOUSE

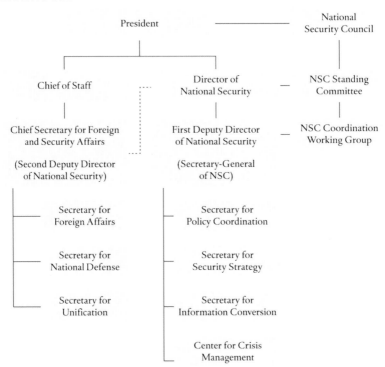

In addition to the president's formalistic style and North Korea's repeated nuclear and missile tests, a shared hard-line policy outlook in foreign and security areas among high-level political appointees discouraged bureaucratic politics. The sole exception was MOU Minister Ryu Gil-jae, a moderate who favored engagement. He often had more lenient interpretations of North Korean behavior than his colleagues and showed more patience in waiting for North Korean responses to proposals of inter-Korean exchanges such as the Trust-Building Process on the Korean Peninsula and the Dresden Initiative.[16] He was replaced as minister in 2015 by Hong Yong-pyo, who had worked for the Park administration as secretary for unification since Park's inauguration; MOU views then fell into line with those of other foreign and security ministries.

RECOMMENDATIONS

Bureaucratic politics in South Korea varied from one administration to the next largely in response to three factors—the president's leadership style, missions of ministries and agencies, and the organizational structure in the Blue House. Among these, the president's leadership style was the most significant.

Some political scientists argue that ideological differences across administrations is also a factor. However, the most pronounced differences were between two progressive presidents—Kim Dae-jung and Roh Moo-hyun. The administrations had another common feature as well: one man (Lim Dong-won and Lee Jong-seok, respectively) dominated foreign and security policy–making. The two were different, however, in their degree of bureaucratic politics, which were more prevalent in the Roh administration. The root of these differences is in the president's leadership style: Kim was more charismatic, popular, and confident in his control over his cabinet and advisors; Roh was more open and fond of policy debates before reaching a decision.

Generally, bureaucratic politics have negative consequences such as inconsistency, poor coordination, and poor timing in making and conducting policy. Several organizational changes could be made to improve decision-making processes in South Korea's executive branch.

- *Simplify the organizational structure of foreign policy–making entities within the Blue House under unified control.* If this step is not taken, then the risk of unnecessary competition and redundancies between the Blue House and ministries remains. Appointees need to be reminded of the importance of coordinated efforts and should be reviewed regularly on their compliance with that goal. The president should refrain from intentionally or inadvertently encouraging competition among advisors and cabinet members. Frequent informal gatherings among heads of relevant ministries and agencies could help strengthen communication and coordination.[17]

- *Establish an office for interagency coordination at the highest level of decision-making.* Like the National Security Council's Standing Committee in the Park administration, a meeting that convenes frequently for consulting and coordinating policies at the ministerial level is most effective. The chair of such a body should be not only knowledgeable about the role but also respected by other members. The president's demonstrated interest in and respect for the resulting policy suggestions is essential, as are candid exchanges of views and resolutions of differences within the body.

- *Diversify methods for recruiting government officials and military officers.* Government agencies and the military should expand recruitment efforts, enhance opportunities for mid-career transitions into public service, and aid in the integration of qualified specialists into selected bureaucratic positions. The current reliance on the civil service examination as the sole vehicle for qualification and staffing of higher positions of government or relying on commissioning military officers from a single military academy limits the pool of qualified individuals available to be considered for senior staff positions.

CONCLUSION

In South Korea, the consequences of bureaucratic politics have differed across issue areas. Any reforms to the decision-making process should keep these differences in mind. In one issue area, the U.S.-ROK alliance, bureaucratic politics have not held much influence. When it comes to the alliance, ideological differences generally have greater influence than bureaucratic politics. Progressive administrations emphasize a more autonomous and independent stance on foreign and security issues and value inter-Korean relations over alliance relations. Conservative administrations tend to do the opposite. Thus, in alliance-related issues, the stance of each administration is a more significant barometer than the positions of ministries and agencies within it.

Foreign and security issues involving countries other than the United States, however, are sometimes influenced by bureaucratic politics, as positions across ministries and agencies differ significantly. In most such cases, differences are between the Ministry of Foreign Affairs and the Ministry of National Defense. The MFA tends to be more cautious and mindful of relations with many different parties, whereas the MND usually prioritizes relations with the United States. However, whether those differences are serious enough to be considered symptoms of bureaucratic politics is debatable.

Policies toward North Korea tend to be affected by bureaucratic politics given the mission of the MOU and the policy outlook of MOU officials. The MOU was established expressly to promote inter-Korean relations and to pursue peaceful unification. MOU staff and officials therefore by definition tend to prefer dialogue and engagement to pressure and confrontation. Meanwhile, the MND and the NIS take tougher stances on and demand more strict reciprocal actions from North Korea. Given these stark differences, policies concerning North Korea are often fractious and poorly coordinated.

As great-power competition in East Asia increases and as the North Korean threat grows, sound foreign and security policy–making in the South Korean government will be critical. The Moon Jae-in administration has a fresh chance at shaping its bureaucratic structure and should carefully examine the experiences of past South Korean administrations to bring forth a coherent policy to benefit the Korean Peninsula as well as the region.

Public Opinion and Presidential Power in South Korea

Jiyoon Kim

Former U.S. Undersecretary of State for Political Affairs Wendy Sherman once lamented that "nationalist feelings can still be exploited, and it's not hard for a political leader anywhere to earn cheap applause by vilifying a former enemy." She then added, "To what extent does the past limit future possibilities for cooperation? The conventional answer to that question, sadly, is a lot."[1] Her remarks came at a time when relations between South Korea and Japan were worsening.

South Korean public opinion has often fueled the country's dismal relations with Japan. Diplomatic relations between the two countries suffer when nationalistic sentiment flares up—particularly around historical issues, such as the controversy surrounding the comfort women statues in front of the Japanese embassy in Seoul and consulate in Busan. Anti-Japanese sentiment among South Koreans, therefore, has been identified by political pundits as a constraint for the nation's government, especially when politicians have made friendly gestures toward Japan. Any reconciliatory moves have been seen as a sign of weakness, thereby limiting Seoul's ability to work with Tokyo. If Sherman is correct, then former President Park Geun-hye vilified an old enemy to gain approval from a public that is still entrenched in the past.

Political scientists and communication scholars have long debated the role of public opinion in policymaking. Theoretical studies, most notably by Benjamin Page and Robert Shapiro, find that public opinion can be rational and worth taking into consideration.[2] Nonetheless, conventional wisdom warns against the dangers of basing policy on public opinion, especially when foreign policy is concerned.

Many pundits and journalists assume that public opinion has a significant influence on policymaking in South Korea. When U.S. soldiers in South Korea accidentally killed two junior high school girls in a roadside accident in 2002, for example, anti-American sentiment spread throughout the nation and arguably decided the outcome of the presidential election that year. In 2008, South Koreans staged massive demonstrations protesting the import of U.S. beef. In 2012, protests forced then President Lee Myung-bak to cancel the General Security of Military Information Agreement (GSOMIA) with Japan just thirty minutes before the scheduled signing.

But such events are the exceptions, not the rule. In fact, the influence of public opinion on the president's decision-making in South Korea is overrated. Although South Korean leaders are sometimes forced to explain their decision-making processes to those who disagree with them, political elites hold significant power to generate, form, influence, and change public opinion. Popular presidents can make decisions and count on their supporters to defend them. Unpopular presidents, however, need to be more careful, as they cannot assume that the same voters who once carried them into office will continue to support their policies.

PUBLIC OPINION AND PRESIDENTIAL DECISIONS

Traditionally, scholars have argued that the average citizen's relative indifference and ignorance of foreign affairs discredit the value of public opinion in the policymaking process. Walter Lippmann and Gabriel Almond have expressed this classical view. Lippmann argues that public opinion sometimes plays a vetoing role against informed and responsible officials making reasonable decisions.[3] Likewise, Almond cited the general public's ignorance of foreign policy as grounds for leaving foreign policy–making to the professionals.[4] The Almond-Lippmann arguments about public opinion have been the conventional wisdom in political science.

Another line of thinking, however, values the wisdom of the public. Benjamin Page and Robert Shapiro assert that, even though individuals can be irrational and often cannot be trusted to make important judgments, the collective body is capable of making reasonably good decisions. They argue that the unstable and random opinions of individuals are dissolved when voices are aggregated.[5]

Yet the rationality of the public can be trusted only to a certain extent. Conventionally, theories assert that individuals do not make independent decisions on political issues. Instead, they look to the political elites they trust. The leading proponent of this theory of elite discourse and public reaction is John Zaller, who argues that people form opinions only after they become aware of the positions of political elites they support. Zaller provides the Vietnam War as an example. During the initial phase of the war, U.S. voters tended to support it because most political elites did. As the opinions of the political elites began to diverge, voters showed similar polarization.[6] George Belknap and Angus Campbell found a similar tendency in the Korean War, a process they described as political heuristics.[7] This line of thinking asserts that members of the general public are too ill-informed to develop their own opinions on political issues. Given policy cues, they may be able to make relatively reasonable decisions, but do so only from time to time.

In fact, the public often fails to understand foreign policy. For instance, when South Koreans were asked about several important agreements between their country and the United States, many responded that they were unaware of them. When asked about the civil-nuclear agreement, which deals with the civilian use of nuclear power and related technological constraints between South Korea and the United States, some 34 percent said they did not know what it was. Only 1.8 percent said that they did know, and 18.5 percent said that they were somewhat aware of the agreement. When asked about the operational control transfer of the South Korean forces by the head of the U.S. Combined Forces Command, which currently holds authority over both U.S. and South Korean forces in times of war, 32.3 percent refused to respond because they did not know the issue well enough. These examples make it clear why many scholars remain wary about government decisions being influenced by public opinion.

Political figures can also sway public opinion on policy issues. One most recent example is free trade, which became an important topic in the 2016 U.S. presidential election. As a candidate, Donald J. Trump and his supporters relentlessly criticized existing free trade agreements and globalization. According to a 2016 poll by the Pew Research Center, only 38 percent of Republicans supported free trade; 53 percent opposed it. On the other side, 56 percent of Democrats supported it and 34 percent opposed. Interestingly, 67 percent of Trump supporters opposed it, 14 percent more than the average Republican rate.[8] Yet just a year earlier, a majority of Republicans had supported it, 53 percent to 35 percent, according to a 2015 survey. Among Democrats in 2015, the numbers were quite similar: 58 percent to 33 percent.[9] Republican opinions on free trade changed significantly over a single year—and, given the particularly high level of opposition among Trump supporters, it is clear how a political figure can influence public opinion.

In South Korea, as in other countries, the public tends to follow the positions of political elites when the issue is divisive. A citizen who supports the president is more likely to support the president's position on a given issue out of loyalty and trust to the officeholder. Therefore, the success or failure of a controversial foreign policy is closely linked with the public's trust in the politicians who propose the policy, particularly the president. When the government's approval ratings are high, even controversial policies are less likely to undermine its popular support. By contrast, unpopular presidents are likely to face a difficult time convincing the public that a given policy is in the country's best interest. This is one reason it is advisable to pursue controversial policies during a president's honeymoon period.

Presidents sometimes make decisions against the wishes of their political base. President Roh Moo-hyun, for instance, sent troops to Iraq on U.S. request despite huge opposition from his progressive supporters. The conservatives, however, given their pro-American tendencies, welcomed the idea. The progressives who vehemently protested the decision eventually had to accept it. Public opinion was split on the issue. Those who supported Roh understood the difficulty of a newly elected South Korean president faced with U.S. pressure, in light of the importance of the United States as an ally.[1] Roh was fortunate to have the conservatives on his side. He was able to negotiate with them easily as he persuaded his own supporters. Thus, it is the president's popularity, the timing of the decision, and whether extra assistance is available that determine a president's political decision.

THE COMFORT WOMEN AGREEMENT

Among the many foreign policies that former President Park Geun-hye pursued, one of the most controversial involved South Korea's relations with Japan. Japanese Prime Minister Shinzo Abe is one of the most widely disliked figures in South Korea. The Abe administration's provocative statements on historical issues have been at the center of the controversy and, as a result, Japan's favorability in South Korea steadily declined from 2010 to 2014.[11] In 2010, Japan's favorability score among

South Koreans was 4.24 out of 10, just a bit worse than China's 4.52. Since then, the score has fallen precipitously. After Park was elected president, Japan's favorability score reached its lowest point, 2.27, in February 2014.[12]

Most South Koreans nonetheless wanted Park to meet with Abe in the hope that relations between Seoul and Tokyo might improve. Even when Japan's favorability score hit bottom in February 2014, 54.9 percent of South Koreans still supported a summit between the two heads of state. Only 38.8 percent opposed it.[13] The South Korean perspective was, in the end, pragmatic. Japan is South Korea's third-largest trading partner and a necessary partner in deterring North Korea. In addition, the U.S. strategy in Northeast Asia, which seeks to use the trilateral relationship to balance China, is widely accepted among the South Korean public as the only way forward. It was, therefore, the Park administration's decision not to meet with Prime Minister Abe until three years into her term.

In 2015, the fiftieth anniversary of the establishment of diplomatic relations between Japan and South Korea, the two sides began to make efforts to repair their relationship. Park and Abe each attended anniversary events in their respective countries. The first summit meeting, if brief, was held that November. Then, in late December, a landmark deal was concluded to resolve the comfort women issue "finally and irreversibly."

Opinion varies little in South Korea about the legacy of sex crimes during World War II. The issue is not only related to human rights, but is also associated with a sense of national responsibility for not having protected Korean girls and women during the war.[14] When the agreement with Japan was first announced, the public greeted the decision with surprise. Media coverage labeled the deal as a breakthrough. With time, however, the specifics of the negotiations became public. That the agreement was deemed final and irreversible and that Japan refused to publicly admit responsibility worsened the situation. The amount of compensation for surviving victims became contentious. Japanese Foreign Minister Fumio Kishida had stated that Japan and South Korea would jointly establish a foundation to provide compensation to the victims. The promised amount totaled slightly less than $10 million, to which many South Koreans took offense, deeming the amount inadequate and refusing to accept it as a gesture of apology. The biggest point of contention, however, was that the Park administration did not consult with the surviving victims before finalizing the agreement.[15] The media and political parties began analyzing the agreement, which led to a divergence of elite opinions. Public opinion soon diverged as well.

DIVIDING ELITES, DIVIDING PUBLIC OPINION

South Korean attitudes toward Japan have rarely been positive, and over the last four years a majority of South Koreans have never rated Japan above 4 on a 1–10 favorability scale. The score for Japan hovered just above 2 in 2013 and 2014, and scores for Prime Minister Abe were even worse. In March of 2014, ratings for Abe (1.11) were lower than those for Kim Jong-un (1.24).[16]

Japan fared slightly better in January 2013, just before Park's inauguration, when it polled at 3.31. Considering that South Korea-Japan relations were not particularly good for the period after Lee Myung-bak's visit to the disputed Dokdo/Takeshima Islands, the score was not as bad as it might have been. The number, however, dropped under Park. During the March 1 presidential address in 2013, the day when South Koreans commemorate the peaceful independence protest that took place more than a century ago, Park took an assertive stance toward Japan and doubled down on her previous antagonism. The media welcomed her remarks. After that, public perception largely followed Park's lead.

In February 2014, in the wake of two major events, Japan's favorability rating plummeted. First, on December 26, 2013, despite opposition from neighboring countries, including South Korea, Prime Minister Abe visited the Yasukuni Shrine—a mid-nineteenth-century Shinto shrine commemorating Japan's war dead, which is controversial because some of those commemorated were deemed by the International Military Tribunal for the Far East to have committed war crimes in World War II. Then on January 28, 2014, the Japanese government approved a history textbook in which the Dokdo/Takeshima island chain—which both South Korea and Japan claim as their own—was described as Japanese territory. Japan's favorability rating hit bottom.

In July 2015, however, public perceptions of Japan spiked among South Koreans following events commemorating the fiftieth anniversary of the normalization of diplomatic relations between the two countries.[17] Events were held in both countries on June 22, Park visiting the Japanese embassy in Seoul and Abe visiting the South Korean embassy in Tokyo. After these visits, many pundits anticipated an improvement in bilateral relations.

What is most notable in the ratings is the clear difference across age groups. When Japan's overall score was at its lowest in February 2014 (2.17), younger South Koreans were most lenient, giving an average score of 2.83 of 10. Those sixty and older were the most critical, giving a score of 1.18. In light of their memories of Japanese colonialism, the elderly have long been the most antagonistic toward Japan and strongly supported Park. When the government has shown signs of reconciliation with Japan, however, the sixty and older age group has been notably receptive. For instance, Japan's favorability score among those in their twenties was 3.76 in June 2015, which improved to 4.14 in July after the fiftieth anniversary events. The score among those in their sixties or older improved by a larger margin, jumping from 2.08 to 2.86 over the same period. The elderly are, at least in part, behind the improving public sentiment toward Japan. Ratings of Japan among South Koreans in their twenties have gradually risen since 2014. Their scores ranged from 2.83 to 4.07 from February 2014 to July 2016. Opinions of those in their fifties and older showed a larger shift, from 1.18 to 3.54 over the same period.

Overall, the public's perception of Japan began to worsen after Park took office in early 2013 and bottomed out in February 2014. Of course, this phenomenon is not solely due to Park's actions. The words and actions of senior Japanese politicians certainly played a role. Some particularly inflammatory remarks came from former Osaka Mayor Toru Hashimoto, who in May 2013 said that the comfort women system was necessary during World War II. Prime Minister Abe himself caused controversy in South Korea when he failed to acknowledge Japanese aggression during the war, saying, "The definition of aggression has yet to be established in academia or in the international community."[18] Nonetheless, perceptions might have been influenced by government actions. Since February 2014, the score has slowly but steadily risen (figure 1). As the South Korean government moved toward reconciliation by exchanging foreign ministers and holding a summit, the public responded in kind, particularly the elderly. But this trend changed with the announcement of the comfort women agreement.

According to an Asan Institute for Policy Studies public opinion poll conducted in January 2016, 51.5 percent of South Koreans disapproved of the new comfort women agreement and 36.2 percent supported it.[19] Generational differences were again notable (figure 2). Approximately

FIGURE 1. JAPAN'S AVERAGE FAVORABILITY SCORES BY AGE GROUP

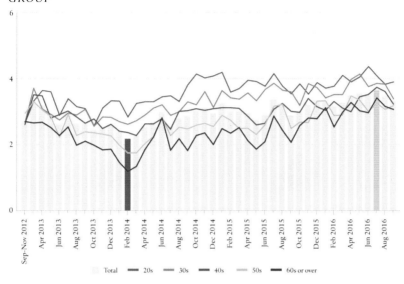

Source: Asan Monthly Poll, 2012–2016.

70 percent of those in their twenties and thirties opposed the deal; only 18.7 percent supported it. The most supportive group was those sixty and older, approximately 59 percent of whom backed the agreement, which came as a surprise given the group's traditional antagonism toward Japan.

Prior to the comfort women agreement, only 56.4 percent of elderly South Koreans supported the idea of cooperation with Japan—a number that leapt to 70.3 percent after the agreement was announced (table 1). South Korean youth reacted differently. Before the agreement, the youth group supported cooperation with Japan. After the announcement, however, that support dropped from 68.7 percent to 61.7 percent. The most likely explanation for this phenomenon is whether a respondent takes political cues from the president. According to a survey conducted by Gallup between January 5 and January 7, 2016, President Park's job approval rating among the elderly was as high as 79 percent, and 54 percent of older South Koreans supported the comfort women agreement—the highest across all age groups. In contrast, just 19 percent of those in their twenties approved of Park's performance, and only 9 percent supported the agreement.[20] The political elite (namely,

FIGURE 2. SUPPORT FOR THE COMFORT WOMEN AGREEMENT BY
AGE GROUP

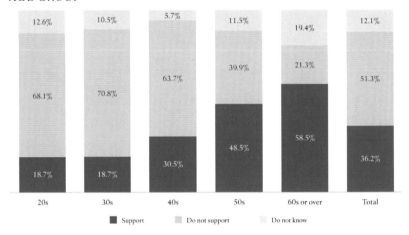

Source: Asan Monthly Poll, January 2016.

the president) were certainly able to mobilize supporters on their side.
Those who support the government and president are therefore likely
to support the government's foreign policy, even if it means reassessing
their political beliefs.

A similar phenomenon is evident in a respondent's ideological tilt
(table 2). Historical issues aside, conservatives were less enthusiastic
about reconciling with Japan. Previously, 65.8 percent of conservatives had supported cooperation with Japan. Liberals were more flexible at 72.6 percent. After the agreement was announced, the numbers
reversed. Among liberals, support dropped to 65.3 percent, and disapproval increased, from 18.7 percent to 27.1 percent. Among conservatives, support increased to 74 percent.

In conclusion, public opinion is influenced by the government's
positions on issues, contrary to the belief of many pundits. The government's positions are best accepted by the public when the sitting administration enjoys high approval ratings. When the government's approval
rating is low, it is hard to garner support, but the government still influences and mobilizes its supporters. Initially, the comfort women agreement generated rancor among the public. The survey results make it
clear that more than a simple majority of South Koreans were unhappy
with the deal. Nevertheless, ten months later, those angry voices qui-
eted and the issue became a bitter memory. One of the reasons public

TABLE 1. SUPPORT FOR COOPERATION WITH JAPAN AFTER THE AGREEMENT BY AGE GROUP

	Cooperation with Japan separate from history issues (before the agreement)			Cooperation with Japan separate from history issues (after the agreement)		
	Approve	Do not approve	Do not know	Necessary	Not necessary	Do not know
20s	68.7%	16.7%	13.1%	61.7%	23.4%	14.9%
30s	65%	22.5%	12.6%	59.1%	26%	14.9%
40s	65.8%	26.0%	7.7%	63.6%	24.6%	11.7%
50s	71.7%	16.6%	11.7%	69.7%	17.5%	12.8%
60s or over	**56.4%**	**21.0%**	21.1%	**70.3%**	**6.9%**	22.1%
Total	65.2%	20.7%	13.4%	65.2%	19.2%	15.5%

Source: Asan Monthly Poll, June 2015; Asan Monthly Poll, January 2016.

TABLE 2. SUPPORT FOR COOPERATION WITH JAPAN AFTER THE AGREEMENT BY IDEOLOGY

	Cooperation with Japan separate from history issues (before the agreement)			Cooperation with Japan separate from history issues (after the agreement)		
	Approve	Do not approve	Do not know	Approve	Do not approve	Do not know
Liberal	**72.6%**	18.7%	8.2%	**65.3%**	27.1%	7.5%
Moderate	68.2%	20.2%	11.4%	63.8%	21.5%	14.3%
Conservative	**65.8%**	23.2%	10.2%	**74.0%**	14.7%	11.3%
Total	65.2%	20.7%	13.4%	65.2%	19.2%	15.5%

Source: Asan Monthly Poll, June 5–6, 2015; Asan Monthly Poll, January 4–5, 2016.

interest in the comfort women agreement dissipated is that the media coverage declined. By April 2016, media outlets had refocused on the National Assembly elections and related issues. In addition, Park's relatively high approval ratings when she announced the agreement helped her and her administration manage the issue without notable protests or objections, except among the youngest voting demographic (figure 3).[21] Having the elderly on her side proved crucial. Public opinion soon shifted in favor of cooperation with Japan, thanks to older voters' defection from the anti-Japan movement.[22]

FIGURE 3. PRESIDENT PARK GEUN-HYE'S APPROVAL RATING

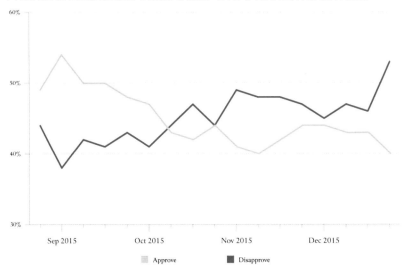

Source: Gallup Korea Daily Opinion, August 2015–January 2016.

Many scholars and pundits suggest that public opinion played a significant role in Park's Japan policy. South Koreans are generally skeptical of Japan, and many in Japan believe that South Koreans are relentlessly pursuing an apology from the Japanese government for crimes committed during World War II. Nonetheless, it is unfair to blame the South Korean public for the country's relations with Japan. South Korean citizens have consistently wanted to forge better relations. The percentage of respondents who support a summit meeting between Park and Abe has always been higher than that of those who do not, and usually tops 50 percent.[23] Many respondents even suggested that Park take a proactive approach to resolving the diplomatic stalemate between the two governments. In December 2013, when the countries' relationship was in deep trouble, 57.8 percent of South Koreans said that President Park should proactively try to improve relations.[24] The public understands that historical issues are difficult to resolve and that the two countries still need each other for practical reasons. It was not the South Korean public that initiated the deadlock in diplomatic relations. It is also not verifiable that anti-Japanese remarks by the South Korean government helped garner public support for the Park administration. It was President Park who unexpectedly made strong and hostile remarks against Japan in her speech on March 1, 2013, just after her inauguration. The South Korean public's favorability score toward Japan then deteriorated, and it took almost two years to bounce back above 3. The public did not ask the president to put the comfort women issue on the table in negotiations with the Japanese government. The issue was one obstacle in South Korean and Japanese relations, but much higher priority was given to the Dokdo/Takeshima Islands dispute and the matter of Japanese textbooks' whitewashing Imperial Japan's colonial and wartime crimes. It was therefore the government's decision, encouraged by Park supporters and particularly the elderly, to go harsh on Japan. Thanks to Park's popularity, this swing toward a more adversarial relationship was well received in South Korea.

THE GSOMIA AND PUBLIC OPINION

In July 2012, the last year of Lee Myung-bak's presidency, South Korea canceled the General Security of Military Information Agreement just half an hour before the scheduled signing. The agreement provided a legal framework for South Korea and Japan to share classified military information about North Korea's nuclear program and China's militarization. When the news broke that South Korea and Japan were about to sign, the government in Seoul was accused by its political opposition—and much of the public—of "selling the country" to its historical enemy. Given that South Korea shares military information with twenty-four other countries, including Russia, the resistance to GSOMIA was not about the principle of sharing intelligence—it was about the country's relationship with Japan.

The Asan Institute public opinion poll, however, makes it clear that GSOMIA was received critically simply because it was declared at the wrong time by the wrong president. Opposition to the deal was largely due to Lee's unpopularity. Lee had enjoyed strong public support until his fourth year. Although his presidency had begun with public protests against U.S. beef imports, his approval rating averaged well over 40 percent in his third year. His fourth year, however, saw those ratings begin to fall. By Lee's fifth year, when GSOMIA was pursued, he was already in his lame duck period. In July 2012, when GSOMIA was canceled, his approval rating was at 23 percent. Because the presidential election was scheduled for December of that year, the ruling Saenuri Party did not defend Lee when the main opposition, the Democratic Party, criticized his administration on GSOMIA.

Although attitudes toward Japan mattered, President Lee's unpopularity was a more significant factor. When both variables were considered together, President Lee's approval ratings had stronger explanatory power than respondents' attitudes toward Japan.[25] A follow-up survey on attitudes toward GSOMIA under President Park revealed strong support for the agreement. Support for GSOMIA reached 60.4 percent in September 2013, and a slim majority remained in favor even after Abe's Yasukuni visit in December (figure 4).[26] Support for GSOMIA also increased in 2016 after North Korea's fifth nuclear test in September of that year. About 65 percent of respondents stated that the GSOMIA with Japan was necessary to counter the North Korean threat; only 25.6 percent said that it was not.[27]

In July 2012, when Lee was facing criticism over GSOMIA, South Koreans in their sixties and above were the most supportive, at 50 percent, and those in their thirties and forties less so, at 40 percent and 40.1 percent, respectively (figure 5). But starting in 2013, support for GSOMIA among younger citizens outpaced support among the elderly. In September 2013, total support for GSOMIA increased to 60.4

FIGURE 4. PUBLIC OPINION ON GSOMIA

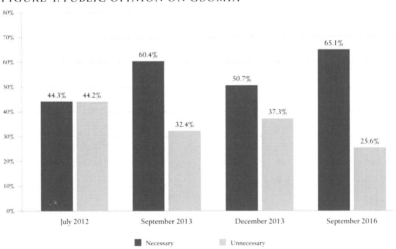

Source: Asan Daily Poll, July 13–15, 2012; Asan Monthly Poll, August 30–September 1, 2013; Asan Monthly Poll, December 29–31, 2013; Asan Monthly Poll, September 21–23, 2016.

FIGURE 5. SUPPORT FOR GSOMIA BY AGE GROUP

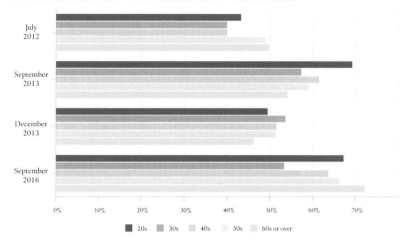

Source: Asan Daily Poll, July 13–15, 2012; Asan Monthly Poll, August 30–September 1; Asan Monthly Poll, December 2013; Asan Monthly Poll, September 2016.

percent thanks to the huge increase in support by those in their twenties. The rate then rose by more than 10 percentage points in all age groups, except for only a 4.3 percentage point increase among respondents in their sixties or over. President Park unleashed her harshest criticism of Japan in 2013, and the countries' relationship hit rock bottom. Park's many elderly supporters sided with her and her government regarding Japan. In December 2013, 46.4 percent of those in their sixties and over supported GSOMIA, the lowest figure across all age groups. In September 2016, however, support among the elderly for GSOMIA rose as high as 72.3 percent, the highest across all age groups. The elderly have been most responsive to the policies of a conservative president: when the president was more accommodating, they were also accommodating. Similarly, when the president's policy was more antagonistic, their position was as well.

RECOMMENDATIONS

Currently, the general public in South Korea has an incredibly positive view of the United States. Since the Asan Institute launched its first annual comprehensive survey in 2010, public support for the U.S.-ROK alliance has never dipped below 90 percent. The highest was recorded in 2013, at 96 percent. Although support for the alliance has been mostly due to practical concerns stemming from North Korea (and China in the long term), a genuinely positive sentiment toward the United States has developed across generations of the South Korean public. The younger generation, in fact, is the most positive toward the United States and most supportive of the U.S.-ROK alliance.

South Korea's relationship with the United States is intrinsically different from its relationship with Japan. Japan is an indispensable trading partner and a de facto security partner, but South Koreans have regularly failed to recognize this significance. They have always considered the United States their most important ally. A large number still believe that the United States plays a critical role in deterring North Korea. Approximately 60 percent of South Koreans see the United States as a more important partner than China.

To maintain cordial relations between South Korea and the United States, the presidents of the two countries need to be determined to maintain a strong alliance. The leaders' words and actions toward each other matter.

To that end, on the Korean side, the Moon Jae-in administration should pursue the following course of action.

- *Consistently show support for the alliance with the United States and for stable relations between South Korea and Japan.* As is clear from the comfort women case, the public tends to follow the lead of political elites they support, even if that means changing their political stances. It is crucial for the heads of state and political elites to show support for alliances and close partners if they seek to maintain good relations with a particular country. The anti-American movement of the past could again prove a difficult obstacle given that public opinion is inherently fickle, and the current sentiment toward the United States is not guaranteed to last. Likewise, a stable South Korea-Japan relationship requires presidential leadership to cultivate a base of support and curb emotional responses to Japan within the Korean public. Any policy or agreement's success or failure largely depends on the popularity of the president or government proposing it. When the president is popular and the government enjoys high levels of trust, it is much easier for them to generate and positively manipulate public opinion to support a policy. However, when the opposite is true, even a reasonably well supported policy can have a hard time being accepted, as was the case with GSOMIA.

On the U.S. side, the Trump administration should aim to accomplish the following goal.

- *Be mindful when discussing South Korea in public.* Anti-American sentiment can flare up if South Koreans feel insulted or disrespected, and President Trump has not spoken highly of South Korea and the U.S.-ROK alliance. His attack on the U.S.-Korea Free Trade Agreement might have aided him in garnering votes, but it generated doubts about the United States among the South Korean public. When he said in interviews that South Korea should pay $1 billion for Terminal High Altitude Area Defense (THAAD) deployment and management, the public image of the United States and its head of state changed for many South Koreans.[28] That episode was eventually smoothed over by his aides, including National Security Advisor H. R. McMaster, but additional remarks by Trump regarding the issue could easily stir up the controversy over THAAD again.

CONCLUSION

In some instances, public opinion can complicate a president's decision-making. However, the ultimate fate of an unpopular foreign policy depends on a president's domestic popularity. In a difficult political period, such as a lame duck period or when faced with low approval ratings, negative public opinion toward the president will work against his or her foreign policy. If a president enjoys a high approval rating and is able to get the support of a solid political base, his or her foreign policy is likely to progress without being challenged.

The scandal surrounding former President Park demonstrates how a president's personal popularity informs the level of popular support for his or her foreign policy objectives. The comfort women agreement, for instance, has been exposed to harsh criticism and is considered to be one of the worst mistakes of the Park administration. The THAAD deployment once received huge support but became a controversial political issue.[29] Furthermore, more than 60 percent of South Koreans now request the National Assembly's ratification of the deployment, which President Moon Jae-in also supports. These challenges are all related to the president's positions and his personal popularity. The Park government's murky decision-making procedures became a serious issue as her popularity declined. As the president became extremely unpopular, people began to criticize her decisions and she was eventually impeached. As a result, the public support for the deployment to go through a ratification procedure in the National Assembly has risen even though the overall level of support for the deployment is higher than the level against it. President Moon—who is enjoying high job approval ratings—is partly responsible for this shift in public opinion.

What was also notable during the impeachment process was the resurrection of Park supporters. In the beginning of the impeachment process, Park was quiet and did not initiate any political actions to defend herself. However, as she began to send messages that she was innocent and had nothing to do with the scandal, and that the impeachment seemed to be a setup, her supporters began to mobilize and protest in large numbers.[30] Even a president with a paltry 4 percent approval rating could encourage and mobilize people to take action; only her most ardent supporters took part. Once her impeachment was finalized and after she disappeared from the political scene, the protesters defending her disappeared as well.

Presidents are also responsible for influencing public opinion. At the very least, a president's strong supporters will likely take his or her side on a given issue. Depending on a president's actions, it is possible for the executive to influence public opinion in a way that could help or obstruct foreign policy–making.

The president and the political elite influence the public more than the public influences the political elite. Before policymakers complain about public opinion having too much influence over foreign policy, they should remind themselves of the responsibility and power in their hands. They may in fact be taking the influence of public opinion more seriously than is merited, perhaps to defend their choices. The ordinary citizen often fails to understand the relevance that foreign policy has in their daily lives. Furthermore, the level and depth of information available to the president is different from what is available to the public. Presidents are well positioned to make foreign policy decisions because they are presented with high-quality information from experts and, most important, they have the advantage as policymakers to make the first move before the relevant information becomes public knowledge. This information dominance provides them with various options. The ability to choose the right time and appropriate way to make foreign policy decisions, while providing a good explanation to the public, is a mark of a president's effectiveness.

Revising South Korea's Constitution

Scott A. Snyder

The impeachment of President Park Geun-hye by parliament in December 2016 and the holding of elections in South Korea in May 2017 have reinvigorated a decade-old debate over whether to revise the country's Sixth Republic Constitution, promulgated as part of the democratic transition in the late 1980s. The constitution has proved effective as a framework to guide South Korean democracy, providing checks and balances that hold the president accountable to the will of the people. But it also is perceived as preserving remnants of South Korea's authoritarian past, including a strong executive authority that some academics have characterized as the "imperial presidency."[1]

South Korea's constitution has provided an effective framework through which the National Assembly has held the president accountable to laws and the will of the people. On two occasions within the last fourteen years, the National Assembly has passed a motion of impeachment against the president. In 2004, the Constitutional Court determined that the impeachment charges against then President Roh Moo-hyun did not justify his removal from office, but acknowledged that his words and actions did not wholly conform to the spirit of the law.[2] The court's verdict illustrated the mix of legal and political factors that the Constitutional Court is empowered to consider as part of its deliberations. In March 2017, the court upheld President Park Geun-hye's removal from office by judging that allegations of bribery and extortion rose to a level that justified her impeachment and subsequent criminal detention. The handling of both cases according to the constitutional framework can be credited as successes for South Korea's democratic system. However, the cases have also shone a spotlight on procedural and structural issues that could be improved through constitutional revision.

The constitutional revision debate that heated up over the past year is likely to continue now that South Korea's domestic situation has stabilized with the election of President Moon Jae-in. Reformers seek to ensure that the constitution promotes efficient governance and can hold the country's political leadership accountable through checks and balances. Given South Korea's vulnerable geopolitical position as a country surrounded by more powerful neighbors, the strength, effectiveness, and resilience of the constitutional framework is all the more important in ensuring the country's political viability. Problems concerning the efficiency of the constitutional framework can generate domestic obstacles that limit South Korea's ability to achieve its full potential as a foreign policy actor in the international system.

ESTABLISHING THE RIGHT
TO A SECOND PRESIDENTIAL TERM

Some South Korean critics of the current constitution would like to remove the single five-year term limit for the presidency, thus allowing an incumbent first-term president to compete for a second term.[3] They argue that such a possibility would reward good presidential performance with the opportunity to remain in office and would establish greater policy continuity and stability.[4]

The removal of the single-term limit on the presidency would improve the effectiveness of the South Korean political leadership by reducing the frequency of transitions from a lame duck presidency to a new administration. It would also allow the continuation of widely accepted policies beyond the two- to three-year window that currently exists when one takes into account the learning curve of a new president and the consequences of a fixed, five-year term on political leadership. The prospect of a second term would provide greater momentum in policymaking by reducing the stagnation and turnover that accompanies a change in presidential leadership every five years. Frequent presidential transitions are usually accompanied by the creation of new policy frameworks or at least the renaming of successful approaches to define them as the product of the new administration. The removal of the single-term limit would promote policy continuity and reward successful performance while minimizing costs and risks of more frequent transitions. At the same time, to earn a second term in office, the incumbent president would have to face the voters and win over their support.

The removal of the one-term presidential limit would likely enhance South Korean foreign policy because countries benefit from experience, continuity, steadiness, and the development of close personal ties among international leaders. Removing the single-term limit would extend the time horizon for pursuing objectives and reduce uncertainty regarding South Korea's foreign policy objectives. It would also reduce the inevitable need by each new South Korean president to reinvent the wheel of policy and governance every five years, a factor that has been a clear constraint on South Korea's ability to reach its full potential as an effective international actor. However, in response to allowing for longer presidential terms, the South Korean public could favor strengthening the National Assembly to provide oversight for public debate on contentious issues regarding domestic and foreign policy. A strengthened National Assembly role in providing oversight over government policies would also be necessary to reduce the risks of an "imperial presidency" that accompany the additional power that might accrue to a president who is able to remain in office for a decade.

DEBATING THE ROLE OF THE PRIME MINISTER

A second area for potential constitutional revision involves the role of the prime minister in the South Korean political system. To strengthen the legitimacy of the designated successor to the president in case of incapacitation or removal from office, one potential improvement would be to replace the prime minister with a vice president who would run with the president on the same ticket. Such a reform would ensure that the successor has a public mandate to exercise political authority in place of the president, as opposed to the current model in which a presidentially appointed prime minister takes power.

A variant of this model would involve holding a separate contest to elect the vice president, thus allowing the vice president and president to represent different parties, as is the case in the Philippines. But this variant would carry clear costs by raising the potential for fragmented leadership and the polarization of political leadership, especially if South Korea were to face future constitutional crises or scandals involving the president.

This issue raises the question of whether the vice president would simply play the role of the prime minister as it is currently established, or if the responsibilities of the vice president would differ significantly. On the one hand, vesting the vice president with a significant level of administrative responsibility could empower the role in ways that would strengthen the sharing of executive responsibilities between the president and vice president, but it could also tie down the vice president and reduce the position's flexibility. On the other hand, if the prime minister's office were abolished and incorporated into the functioning of the Blue House (the official residence of the South Korean head of state), the executive authority and administrative control of South Korea's president would conceivably be strengthened. In reality, however, Blue House political directives have always bypassed and superseded those of the office of the prime minister.

An alternative would be to introduce a hybrid model, similar to the French political system, in which a prime minister exercises control over domestic affairs and a president represents the nation on matters of national security and foreign policy.

On paper, a dual leadership system appears to be an efficient way of dividing domestic and international policy responsibilities into manageable roles that would enable the offices of the prime minister and the president to efficiently share power and concentrate on their respective responsibilities in loose cooperation with each other. But a potential weakness of this model is the challenge of power sharing and the possibility that a dual leadership system, if imported to a South Korean political context, would induce competition rather than cooperation among political leaders. South Korea's historical experience with leadership tends toward a unitary model in which the chief decision-maker not only does not share power, but also fails to work with potential successors in fear that they could become challengers for political power.

If a hybrid system were to prove workable in South Korea, the division of domestic and international responsibilities could result in a more effective implementation of South Korean foreign policy. But if the president and the prime minister end up competing with each other for dominance, the hybrid system would become a source of weakness and distraction that would inhibit South Korea from achieving its international potential.

BALANCING EXECUTIVE
AND LEGISLATIVE POWER

For those who view the current constitution as allowing an overly strong executive authority that could lead to the imperial presidency phenomenon, a natural antidote would be to empower the National Assembly's checking functions on executive power. Under South Korea's current system, the roles and responsibilities of the National Assembly are considerably more limited vis-à-vis the executive than the powers that Congress enjoys in the U.S. system. For instance, in South Korea, the main responsibilities for setting the government budget and initiating legislation lie primarily within the executive branch, and the National Assembly only holds the right to pass or reject relevant legislation.

Traditionally, members of the National Assembly initiate only a small proportion of the legislation that they consider for approval. The National Assembly holds hearings to vet cabinet ministers nominated by the president, but does not have the power to reject the nominations. Instead, confirmation hearings generate public reactions that can affect the president's approval ratings, but the president is not constitutionally bound to follow the National Assembly or public opinion. Likewise, the National Assembly performs regular audits and inspection activities designed to hold specific branches of the government to account, but it does not constitutionally hold the power of the purse. One effect of the National Assembly's relatively limited responsibilities is that it can indirectly enhance the temptation of individual members to grandstand on particular issues rather than taking responsible positions as part of the public debate. Constitutional revision would be an opportunity to restrain executive authority in part by empowering the National Assembly to serve as a more effective check on presidential prerogatives. The authority of the National Assembly could be increased by strengthening legislative budgetary authority, enhancing legislative oversight of executive functions, and empowering the National Assembly with the right to reject presidential nominees to cabinet-level positions in the government.

A stronger oversight role for the National Assembly would likely have mixed effects on South Korean foreign policy. The ability of the president to formulate and implement foreign policy is currently relatively unconstrained by legislative factors, although South Korea's democratic transition has strengthened the influence of public opinion on foreign policy formation. For instance, democratization has enabled voices of opposition to organize and mobilize on sensitive foreign policy issues, such as the public demonstrations in 2008 against the Lee Myung-bak administration's approval of expanded U.S. beef imports as a result of (unfounded) public fears surrounding mad cow disease.[5] The National Assembly became a focal point for public demonstrations because of its role in ratifying the U.S.-Korea Free Trade Agreement in 2011, but a weak National Assembly means that the legislature plays a marginal role in influencing the formation and implementation of South Korea's foreign policy. Strengthened budgetary, oversight, and legislative roles for the National Assembly in a revised constitution would grant the legislature more power over foreign policy–making. These changes would also enhance the public accountability of South Korea's foreign policy by adding stronger oversight in addition to the ongoing need for broad public support. But a strengthened legislative role, while enhancing public accountability, could potentially limit South Korea's foreign policy effectiveness if public opinion is influenced by volatile hot-button issues rather than long-term national strategies.

THE MERITS AND RISKS OF A PARLIAMENTARY SYSTEM

Another element of South Korea's debate over constitutional revision asks whether the country would be better served by a weaker executive coupled with a parliamentary system. In this scenario, the leader of the ruling party would become prime minister and appoint a cabinet from members of his or her party. Prime ministerial systems are lauded by political scientists as more efficient than presidential systems, and this revision would eliminate concerns about the imperial presidency. A parliamentary system would also reduce the prospect of a divided government and political gridlock in which a president from a minority party has to work with a National Assembly controlled by the opposition. But the South Korean public has consistently shown strong support for a presidential system, perhaps in part because such a system highlights the role of direct democracy through a vote for the leader versus indirect democracy in which public preferences are intermediated by the selection of a leader from within the national legislature.

If South Korea were to have a parliamentary system, the closest model for how such a system would play out in practice would be Japan, the difference being that South Korea's legislature is unicameral rather than bicameral. However, scholars have expressed concern about enacting such a system in South Korea, where a pull toward factionalism and so-called boss politics in which parties become dominated by strong individuals who exert control and impose party discipline is entirely possible. In a boss politics model, leaders of competing entourages compete for control of government in a fashion similar to the role that factional groupings have played in parliamentary politics in Japan. Such a system could lead to a succession of weak leaders and frequent changes of the prime minister, thus weakening the continuity and duration of political leadership. A parliamentary system might generate frustrations among a public that perceives direct democracy as the process that most effectively empowers public choice and maximizes the influence of public opinion on political leadership.

A parliamentary system could also potentially vest greater power in organized political parties, which have traditionally been the least accountable and most distrusted actors in South Korean politics. The risk, therefore, is that South Korean politicians would continue to be perceived as treating politics as a parlor game designed primarily to serve special interests or pursue personal ambitions rather than as showing accountability to the broader public.

If the adoption of a parliamentary system resulted in frequent changes in leadership and a revolving-door cabinet system, then South Korea's international clout would likely diminish. However, its foreign policy effectiveness might flourish under a prime minister who can muster the requisite political leadership to sustain support and provide continuity and stability for the nation's foreign policy objectives.

STRENGTHENING LOCAL AUTONOMY AND GOVERNANCE

South Korea's political system was highly centralized when the country was under authoritarian rule. Decentralization and the establishment of local governance have occurred gradually following South Korea's democratic transition. The central government still exercises a great deal of influence over local autonomy and political structures through its ability to issue administrative guidance (similar to executive orders) that constrain the autonomy of local political actors. In addition, although local governments have made progress in securing budgetary authority over projects within their purview, central government control over financing decisions can still influence the situation at the local level, providing the central government with significant leverage. If constitutional reforms were to strengthen local autonomy by more strongly endorsing decentralization, power between the central and local governments could be shifted in ways that provide local governments with greater authority on specific international issues that require their cooperation.

Stronger local autonomy could enhance mechanisms of accountability in foreign policy, but struggles between empowered local authorities and the central government can also result in political gridlock. For instance, the reconfiguration and consolidation of U.S. Forces Korea (USFK) has resulted in a complicated interaction with local and provincial governments in South Korea as former USFK bases are vacated and turned over to local authorities in northern areas of Gyeonggi Province, such as Dongducheon, and local communities near Osan-Pyeongtaek have had to grapple with the implications of a larger U.S. military presence in their communities. Strengthening local autonomy by constitutional revision would likely give even greater voice to communities on specific foreign policy issues requiring local cooperation such as the scope and environment for sustaining U.S. forces in South Korea. The consequences of enhanced local autonomy on South Korean foreign policy need not be detrimental, but could constrain the ability of the foreign ministry to effectively manage some foreign policy issues without close consultation and support from local authorities, especially those whose communities are directly affected by the issue concerned.

RECOMMENDATIONS

To the extent that the constitution provides a framework and context for effective implementation of state policy, a properly structured constitution that enables accountability and efficiency in the conduct of state affairs will maximize state interests and the capacity to conduct foreign policy. Constitutional reformers should aim to accomplish the following objectives.

- *Implement a two-term presidential system.* South Korea's presidential system provides greater continuity of representation and consistency in the conduct of international affairs than is likely to occur in a parliamentary system. But the current single-term limit necessitates a complete reordering of personnel and priorities under each newly elected president. South Korea could achieve a stronger international profile and smoother implementation of its foreign policy with a two-term presidential system than with a mandatory one-term limit.

- *Strengthen the oversight roles and influence of the National Assembly.* A stronger National Assembly would impose limits on the power of the presidency and provide greater public accountability in many policy areas, including foreign policy. The National Assembly already provides a measure of public accountability to the executive branch in foreign policy by calling frequent hearings at which cabinet-level ministers are required to appear and explain the objectives, strategies, and management of the country's foreign policy. The oversight role of the National Assembly should be further strengthened as the primary way to provide public accountability of the executive in foreign policy.

- *Streamline election schedules.* A South Korean constitutional revision effort will also need to harmonize the presidential, legislative, and local election cycles to make elections more efficient and predictable. The current system—in which the president is elected every five years, the legislature is elected every four years, and local elections are held every three years—is wasteful and confusing. The procedures and processes for handling presidential impeachment could also be reviewed to ensure continuity of governance and to provide greater details regarding the succession of authority. Streamlining South Korea's election schedule and alignment of presidential and legislative elections would generate a greater sense of predictability in South Korea's politics. This could also enhance stability in the domestic political environment, thereby enhancing the potential for continuity in the handling of foreign policy.

CONCLUSION

The recent constitutional crisis and the impeachment of Park Geun-hye catalyzed renewed discussion of constitutional revision in South Korea. The immediate crisis has passed, but the issues raised in the course of the crisis deserve careful consideration. Constitutional revision should not become a political football that various parties use in an attempt to reshape the South Korean political landscape. The time frame for implementing proposals for constitutional revision needs to be divorced from the immediate political calendar so that no actor can turn the discussion to gain immediate political advantage.

South Korea's Sixth Republic Constitution has adequately managed the country's democratic transition and consolidation over the past two decades. However, calls have been persistent to address structural and procedural flaws that have hindered South Korea from achieving its full potential and from maintaining the continuity necessary to support long-term policy objectives while also holding individuals accountable. These constitutional reforms could enhance the accountability, stability, and efficiency of South Korea's politics.

Endnotes

STRENGTHENING THE NATIONAL ASSEMBLY'S INFLUENCE ON SOUTH KOREAN FOREIGN POLICY

1. See Barbara Hinckley, *Less Than Meets the Eye: Foreign Policy Making and the Myth of the Assertive Congress* (Chicago: University of Chicago Press, 1994).
2. See James M. Lindsay, *Congress and the Politics of U.S. Foreign Policy* (Baltimore: Johns Hopkins University Press, 1994).
3. Young-gook Jung, "Uighoe Jungchiwa Oegyojungchaek" (Politics in the National Assembly and Foreign Policy), *Euijung Yeongu* (Korean Journal of Legislative Studies), no. 2 (1996): 142.
4. The Grand National Party published a report criticizing the transition team for making conflicts with government agencies. See Young-shik Goo, "Transition Team, Forcefully Seeking to Change Basic Policy," *OhmyNews*, February 10, 2003, http://news.naver .com/main/read.nhn?mode=LSD&mid=sec&sid1=100&oid=047&aid=0000024146.
5. Sang-yong O, "(EDaily Report) The Age of Outcasts," *EDaily*, February 12, 2003, http://news.naver.com/main/read.nhn?mode=LSD&mid=sec&sid1=101&oid=018& aid=0000005562.
6. Jin-wook Choi, "Lee Myung-bak Jeongbueui Daebuk Jeongchaekgwa Bukhaneui Baneung" (North Korea Policy of Lee Myung-bak Administration and North Korea's Responses), *Tongil Jeongchaek Yeongu* (International Journal of Korean Unification Studies) 17, no. 1 (2008): 54, footnote 12.
7. Robert Putnam, "Diplomacy and Domestic Politics: The Logic of Two Level Games," *International Organization* 42, no. 3 (1988): 427–60.
8. The Japan-Korea Parliamentarians' Union was established in 1972, and the former chairmen of the union in each country such as Jong-pil Kim, Tae-joon Park, and Sang-deuk Lee on the South Korean side and Mori Yoshiro and Fukuda Takeo on the Japanese side played important roles in discussing the different opinions between the two countries when the bilateral relationship deteriorated.
9. The share of the foreign ministry budget for Canada is 2 percent of the government's budget. It is 4.08 percent for the Netherlands, and 7.2 percent for Spain as of 2015. The number of personnel employed by the foreign ministries of those countries is also much higher than in South Korea. Canada employs 7,200, the Netherlands 3,164, and Spain 2,743, whereas South Korea employs 2,188, according to the National Inspection Material from the office of Moon Hee-sang (member of the National Assembly, the Minjoo Party of Korea, October 13, 2016).

BUREAUCRATIC POLITICS IN SOUTH KOREAN FOREIGN POLICY–MAKING

1. Graham T. Allison, *Essence of Decision: Explaining the Cuban Missile Crisis* (Boston: Little, Brown, 1971), 144.

2. They include Kim Ki-jung, "South Korean North Korea Policy and Bureaucratic Politics," *National Strategy* 4, no. 1 (1998): 5–46; Jong-yun Bae, "Korean Foreign Policy With the Bureaucratic Politics Model: Its Reliability and Usefulness," *Korea Journal of International Politics* 42, no. 4 (2002): 97–116; "Bureaucratic Politics and Korean Foreign Policy on North Korea in 1990s," *Korean Journal of Political Science* 37, no. 5 (2003), 147–65; Sung-deuk Hahm and Okjin Kim, "Presidential Leadership and Bureaucratic Politics in Foreign Policy–Making Process of Korea: Cases of North Korean Nuclear Crisis I and II," *Journal of International Relations Studies* 10, no. 2 (2005): 37–70; Moon-suk Ahn, "The Analysis of South Korean Foreign Policy Making in the Wake of the North Korean Nuclear Test: The Application of Bureaucratic Politics Model," *Korean Journal of Political Science* 42, no. 1 (2008): 207–26; and "Bureaucratic Politics and Mobilization of Power Resources by Bureaucrats," *Korean Journal of International Politics* 55, no. 4 (2015): 169–201.

3. Bae, "Korean Foreign Policy," and Kim, "South Korean North Korea Policy" are informative.

4. In distinguishing the presidential leadership styles, Alexander George used three criteria: the president's cognitive style, sense of efficacy, and orientation toward political conflict (*Presidential Decision-Making in Foreign Policy: The Effective Use of Information and Advice* [Boulder, CO: Westview Press, 1980], 108–18). For more discussions of leadership style and its influence on policymaking, see Margaret G. Hermann, Charles F. Hermann, and Joe D. Hagan, "How Decision Units Shape Foreign Policy Behavior," *New Directions in the Study of Foreign Policy*, ed. C. F. Hermann, C. W. Kegeley Jr., and J. N. Rosenau (Boston: Allen & Unwin, 1987), 309–36; and William W. Newmann, "The Structures of National Security Decision Making: Leadership, Institutions, and Politics in the Carter, Reagan, and G. H.W. Bush Years," *Presidential Studies Quarterly* 34, no. 2 (2004): 272–306.

5. For detailed descriptions of the innate missions of the major ministries and agencies relevant to foreign and security policies in South Korea, see Kim, "South Korean North Korea Policy."

6. The name for the agency charged with collecting and analyzing intelligence and information, investigating espionage activities, running counterintelligence operations, and so on has changed a few times since its creation. This paper uses the most recent—NIS—to apply throughout.

7. Alliance-first thinking may be treated as a structural factor for another reason: at both the Ministry of National Defense and the Ministry of Foreign Affairs, the bureaus in charge of U.S. affairs are the central units in terms of mission and personnel affairs. People who have worked in those bureaus are usually guaranteed a promotion.

8. For a detailed historical review and discussion on foreign and security policy–making systems of different administrations, see Sung-bae Kim, Ho-ryung Lee, Jae-sung Chun, and Kang Choi, *A Desirable Decision-Making System of Foreign and Security Policy for South Korea*, 2013 EAI Special Report (Seoul: East Asia Institute, 2013); and Bong-geun Jeon, "A Historical Review of National Security Policy Controlling Systems and Office of National Security of South Korea," *Weekly Analysis*, no. 2013-03 (Seoul: Institute for Foreign Affairs and National Security, 2013).

9. His treatment of the NSC was little different: meetings were convened only three times during his five-year term.
10. For Kim Young-sam's leadership style, see Hahm and Kim, "Presidential Leadership," and Park Yong-soo, "The Competitive Foreign Policy Management Style of the President Kim Young-sam in the Process of First North Korean Nuclear Crisis," *Korean Journal of International Politics* 55, no. 4 (2015): 139–68.
11. As Kim Dae-jung's term advanced and Lim's job position changed, however, Lim's control over foreign and security policy areas weakened, and thus bureaucratic politics became more common.
12. For explanation of this case in detail, see Bae, "Korean Foreign Policy."
13. For Roh's leadership style, see Hahm and Kim, "Presidential Leadership"; Ahn, "Analysis of South Korean"; Park Yong-suk, "The Second North Korean Nuclear Issue and Roh Moo-hyun's Leadership," *Journal of Asia Studies* 56, no. 3 (2013): 231–65.
14. As revealed during the impeachment process of President Park, this characteristic can be controversial because Choi Soon-sil, who is known as Park's closest confidant, appears to have played an influential role in some important policy decisions. Judging from many of the tough decisions that Park had to make throughout her long political career, however, she seems to have tried at least to maintain consistency in her decisions.
15. For Park's leadership style, see Ahn, "Bureaucratic Politics."
16. For the consequences that resulted from Ryu's different policy outlook, see Ahn, "Bureaucratic Politics."
17. For more detailed discussions on a better decision-making system of national security policy for South Korea, see S. Kim et al., *A Desirable Decision-Making System*; Jeon, "A Historical Review."

PUBLIC OPINION AND PRESIDENTIAL POWER IN SOUTH KOREA

1. Kang Seung-woo, "U.S. Takes Sides With Japan on History Issue," *Korea Times*, March 1, 2015, http://koreatimes.co.kr/www/news/nation/2015/03/116_174379.html.
2. Benjamin I. Page and Robert Y. Shapiro, *The Rational Public: Fifty Years of Trends in Americans' Policy Preferences* (Chicago: University of Chicago Press, 1992).
3. Walter Lippmann, *Essay in the Public Philosophy* (New York: New American Library, 1958).
4. Gabriel A. Almond, "Public Opinion and National Security Policy," *Public Opinion Quarterly* 20, no. 2 (Summer 1956), 371–78.
5. Page and Shapiro assert that the "public, as a collectivity, holds a number of real, stable, and sensible opinions about public policy, and that these opinions develop and change in a reasonable fashion, responding to changing circumstances and to new information" (*Rational Public*, 1).
6. See John Zaller, *The Nature and Origins of Mass Opinion* (Cambridge: Cambridge University Press, 1992).
7. See George Belknap and Angus Campbell, "Political Party Identification and Attitudes Toward Foreign Policy," *Public Opinion Quarterly* 15, no. 4 (December 1951), 601–23.
8. Bruce Stokes, "Republicans, Especially Trump Supporters, See Free Trade Deals as Bad for U.S.," Pew Research Center, March 31, 2016, http://pewresearch.org/fact-tank/2016/03/31/republicans-especially-trump-supporters-see-free-trade-deals-as-bad-for-u-s/.

9. "Free Trade Agreements Seen as Good for U.S., but Concerns Persist," Pew Research Center, May 27, 2015, http://people-press.org/2015/05/27/free-trade-agreements-seen-as-good-for-u-s-but-concerns-persist/.

10. The public opinion poll was conducted by the progressive newspaper *Hankyoreh* on October 18 and 19, 2003. The sample size was seven hundred. In the survey, 56.6 percent of respondents supported the decision to send troops to Iraq and 41.6 percent opposed it. The main reason for supporting the decision was strengthening the U.S.-ROK alliance facing the North Korean threat. See "National Public Opinion Survey on the Decision to Send Troops to Iraq," *Hankyoreh*, October 20, 2003, http://legacy.www.hani.co.kr/section-007003000/2003/10/007003000200310200136001.html.

11. The Japanese side may attribute this to former President Lee Myung-bak's visit to Dokdo.

12. Annual survey of the Asan Institute for Policy Studies, 2010–2012. Asan Monthly Surveys in 2013, 2014, 2015, and 2016.

13. Asan Monthly Survey February 1–3, 2014; Asan Monthly Survey February 23–25, 2014.

14. Those who are in their twenties are slightly more sensitive to this issue than other generations.

15. Among those who oppose the agreement, 48.1 percent said that the government should be blamed for not having consulted with surviving comfort women before it reached the agreement.

16. Public opinion data from the Asan Institute for Policy Studies. Favorability ratings for head of states have been tracked by the Asan Institute's monthly survey since 2013. The survey in which Prime Minister Abe's favorability score was even lower than Kim Jong-un's was conducted February 1–3, 2014. All surveys consist of randomly collected samples of one thousand people nationwide with a 3.1 percent margin of error. The survey was done by landline and mobile telephone.

17. The favorability score for Japan increased to 3.39 in July 2015. The lowest score is 2.17, which was recorded in February 2014. Asan Institute conducted the survey between February 1 and February 3, 2014, and again between July 1 and July 3, 2015.

18. Kirk Spitzer, "Sorry, But Japan Still Can't Get the War Right," *Time*, May 20, 2013, http://nation.time.com/2013/05/20/sorry-but-japan-still-cant-get-the-war-right/.

19. Asan Institute survey conducted January 1–3, 2016.

20. "Daily Opinion Number 193 (First Week of January 2016)," Gallup Korea, January 7, 2016, http://gallup.co.kr/gallupdb/reportContent.asp?seqNo=720.

21. Park's approval ratings were around 40 percent despite several political scandals. They dipped as low as 30 percent at times, such as when the Middle East Respiratory Syndrome crisis broke out, the Sewol ferry sank, and fellow party member Yoo Seung-min was expelled from the floor leadership. Yet after each crisis her ratings promptly bounced back to the 40 percent level. She faced protests and objections by progressive NGOs, young South Koreans, and opposition parties, but they did not rise to a serious level, partly because President Park still maintained decent approval ratings, and the opposition was preoccupied with the upcoming general election.

22. Park's solid approval ratings started to slip away after the twentieth National Assembly elections, in which the Saenuri Party suffered a major defeat. After the defeat, Park released a statement that did not reflect critically on her time in office, and simply interpreted the election result as a warning to the National Assembly to work more efficiently and harder, angering the public.

23. The lowest approval of the summit was 49.5 percent in December 2013, but it was still higher than the disapproval rate (40.7 percent). In 2014 and 2015, support for the summit was 54.9 percent and 56.3 percent, respectively. Asan Daily Poll, December 29–31, 2013; February 23–25, 2014; Asan Monthly Poll, June 9–10, 2015.

24. Asan Daily Poll, December 29–31, 2013.

25. President Lee Myung-bak's job approval ratings in the last year of his term were about 24 percent on average. According to Gallup, his approval rating for the third quarter (July–September) was 23 percent. His disapproval rating was 59 percent. See Gallup Korea Daily Opinion, no. 193, January 5–6, 2016. A more detailed analysis is found in the report published by the Asan Institute. See Karl Friedhoff and Choongku Kang, "Rethinking Public Opinion on Korea-Japan Relations," *Issue Brief*, Asan Institute for Policy Studies, October 14, 2013, http://en.asaninst.org/contents/issue-brief-no-73-rethinking-public-opinion-on-korea-japan-relations/.

26. Asan Institute surveys conducted between August 30 and September 1 and December 29–31, 2013.

27. Asan Institute survey conducted on September 21–23, 2016. The question's wording was different from previous surveys in the addition of the "for the preparation of North Korea's nuclear threat" condition. Thus it is possible that respondents were more likely to answer that it was necessary.

28. James Pearson and Ju-min Park, "Trump's Demand Seoul Pay for THAAD Will Test Ties as Moon Presidency Looms," Reuters, April 28, 2017, http://reuters.com/article/US-usa-trump-southkorea-analysis-idUSKBN17U13O.

29. A public opinion poll conducted by *Korea Times* (February 24–25) indicates that 46.9 percent supported the THAAD deployment, and 36 percent opposed. The decrease in opposition was driven by various factors such as the Park impeachment and China's retaliation to THAAD. See Park Jin-man, "THAAD Deployment: Support 47% Oppose 36%," *Korea Times*, February 27, 2017, http://hankookilbo.com/v/2c6497be8dc64aba9c3440073537efoe.

30. Park threw a sudden New Year press conference on January 2 and gave an interview on a conservative internet news outlet, Jung Kyu Jae TV.

REVISING SOUTH KOREA'S CONSTITUTION

1. Cho Hae-jin, "An Imperial Presidency Must Stop," *Korea JoongAng Daily*, October 25, 2014, http://koreajoongangdaily.joins.com/news/article/article.aspx?aid=2996446.

2. James Brooke, "Constitutional Court Reinstates South Korea's Impeached President," *New York Times*, May 14, 2004, http://nytimes.com/2004/05/14/world/constitutional-court-reinstates-south-korea-s-impeached-president.html?_r=0.

3. Kim Hyo-jin, "Constitutional Reform Takes Center Stage," *Korea Times*, December 19, 2016, http://koreatimes.co.kr/www/news/nation/2016/12/180_220446.html.

4. AFP-JJ et al., "South Korean Leader Proposes Revising Constitution to Let President Serve More Than One Term," *Japan Times*, October 24, 2016, http://japantimes.co.jp/news/2016/10/24/asia-pacific/politics-diplomacy-asia-pacific/south-korea-leader-proposes-revising-presidential-system/.

5. Choe Sang-hun, "Beef Protest Turns Violent in South Korea," *New York Times*, June 30, 2008, http://nytimes.com/2008/06/30/world/asia/30korea.html.

Acknowledgments

The CFR program on U.S.-Korea Policy would like to acknowledge and thank the Korea Foundation and the Smith Richardson Foundation for their support of this project. Most important, the program is grateful to the volume's Korean authors, who presented initial drafts of their chapters at a June 2016 conference held at CFR's Washington, DC, office. The program is also grateful for the continued contribution of programmatic support to CFR from the Korea International Trade Association. CFR Senior Vice President and Director of Studies James M. Lindsay and Editorial Director Patricia Dorff provided valuable editorial comments that strengthened this project, and Associate Editor Erik Crouch and Assistant Editor Sumit Poudyal ably edited and managed the production of this publication. Finally, I would like to thank my research associate, Sungtae "Jacky" Park, for his skill in managing the project and the publication process.

Scott A. Snyder
January 2018

About the Authors

Scott A. Snyder is senior fellow for Korea studies and director of the U.S.-Korea Policy program at the Council on Foreign Relations (CFR), where he served as an adjunct fellow from 2008 to 2011. Prior to joining CFR, Snyder was a senior associate in the international relations program of the Asia Foundation, where he founded and directed the Center for U.S.-Korea Policy. He also served as the Asia Foundation's representative in South Korea from 2000 to 2004. Previously, he was a senior associate at the Pacific Forum Center for Strategic International Studies. He has worked as an Asia specialist at the United States Institute of Peace and as acting director of Asia Society's contemporary affairs program. He serves as co-chair of the advisory council of the National Committee on North Korea. Snyder is author and editor of numerous books on Korean foreign policy and politics. His new book is *South Korea at the Crossroads: Autonomy and Alliance in an Era of Rival Powers*. He received a BA in English and history from Rice University and an MA in East Asian studies from Harvard University.

Geun Lee is a professor at the Graduate School of International Studies and dean of the Office of International Affairs at Seoul National University. He is a member of the Regional Governance Council at the World Economic Forum, and was formerly the chairman of the forum's Global Agenda Council on the future of Korea. Lee is the chief vision officer at the Mirezi (Future Insight) think tank. He was formerly a professor at the Institute of Foreign Affairs and National Security at the Republic of Korea's Ministry of Foreign Affairs and Trade, and a consultative committee member at the ROK Ministry of Foreign Affairs. Formerly he was president of the Korea Institute for Future Strategies and director at the Institute of International Affairs at Seoul National University. He received a BA in political science from Seoul National University and an MA and a PhD in political science from the University of Wisconsin, Madison.

Young Ho Kim is a professor of international relations at Korea National Defense University (KNDU) in Seoul. He has served as the director of KNDU's Center for Security Policy and Center for U.S. and China Affairs, as chair of the Department of International Relations, and as head of the Division of International Affairs at the Research Institute for National Security Affairs. From 2014 to 2016 he served in the ROK presidential office as deputy secretary to the president for security strategy. Previously, he served as a policy advisor to the chief secretary to the president for foreign policy and security. Kim received a BA in international relations from Yonsei University and an MA and a PhD in political science from Ohio State University.

Jiyoon Kim is a research fellow in the Public Opinion Studies Program in the Center for Public Opinion and Quantitative Research at the Asan Institute for Policy Studies. Previously, Kim was a postdoctoral research fellow at Université de Montréal. Her research interests include elections and voting behavior, American politics, and political methodology. Her recent publications include "Political Judgment, Perceptions of Facts, and Partisan Effects" (with Andre Blais), "The Party System in Korea and Identity Politics," and "Cognitive and Partisan Mobilization in New Democracies: The Case of South Korea." She received a BA from Yonsei University, an MPP in public policy from the University of California, Berkeley, and a PhD in political science from the Massachusetts Institute of Technology.